Thinking the Unthinkable

The Unexplained
Mysteries of Mind Space
and Time

Thinking the Unthinkable

Ideas which have upset conventional thought

Editor: Peter Brookesmith

Orbis Publishing · London

Acknowledgements

Photographs were supplied by Aldus Books, American Museum of Natural History, Associated Press, A–Z Botanical Collection, Chris Barker, T.E. Bearden, Paul Brierley, Brown Bros., C.E.G.B., Jean-Loup Charmet, Bruce Coleman, Cooper Bridgeman Library, J. Cutten, Philip Daly, Arnold Desser, Sam Elder, Mary Evans Picture Library, Flicks, Werner Forman Archive, Leif Geiges, Institute of Geological Sciences, Giraudon, Henry Gris, Harvard News Office, High Times, Toby Hogarth, Michael Holford, Imitor, Keystone Press Agency, Kobal Collection, Laing Art Gallery, London Scientific Fotos, Dr. J.A. Macrae, Mansell Collection, NASA, National Gallery of Canada, Peter Newarks–Western Americana, Novosti, Oxford Scientific Films, Guy Lyon Playfair, Popperfoto, Ann Ronan, Rex Features, Scale, Prof. G. Schatten, Science Museum, Science Photo Library, Ronald Sheridan Picture Library, P. Snelgrove, Space Frontiers, Spectrum, B. Stewart, Sunday Times, Theosophical Publishing Co., Sally Ann Thompson, John Topham Picture Library, UPI, USAF, Vautier de Nanxe, John Walsh, Yorkshire TV.

Consultants to The Unexplained
Professor A. J. Ellison
Dr J. Allen Hynek
Brian Inglis
Colin Wilson

Editorial Director
Brian Innes

Editor
Peter Brookesmith

Deputy Editor
Lynn Picknett

Executive Editor
Lesley Riley

Sub Editors
Mitzi Bales
Chris Cooper
Jenny Dawson
Hildi Hawkins

Picture Researchers
Anne Horton
Paul Snelgrove
Frances Vargo

Editorial Manager
Clare Byatt

Art Editor
Stephen Westcott

Designer
Richard Burgess

Art Buyer
Jean Hardy

Production Co-ordinator
Nicky Bowden

Volume Editor
Lorrie Mack

Assistants
Ruth Turner
Sarah Reason

Contents

Introduction

IT IS A HABIT OF THOUGHT in the civilised world to believe that ours is a rational and tolerant society. We enjoy free speech, a free press and democratic rule.

Yet in certain respects we are as primitive as we ever were, for all our technological sophistication. Our very belief that we have found out most of the answers to most of the questions about the world could be considered a superstition as great as any hope entertained by a simple tribesman that dancing will bring rain in the dry season. Equally primitive is the idea that we are prepared to tolerate radically new ideas.

If this seems an unwarranted attack on modern 'civilised' society, let us look at a couple of examples. If, for instance, it were true that science has discovered most of the truth about the world we live in, how is it that scientists are discovering new truths every day? But surely, it might be objected, if that's the case, then how can it be said that we are intolerant of new ideas? Aren't scientists, of all people, constantly taking in new ideas and applying them faster than anyone else?

To some extent the answer to this is yes. But the new ideas they are willing to accept don't challenge their most cherished thinking. Truly original thought takes a remarkably long time to displace the old forms, and one highly original thinker is not necessarily tolerant of the notions of another.

Take the case of the two geniuses of modern physics, Albert Einstein and Werner Heisenberg. Einstein's theory of relativity had caused scientists to view the nature of space and time in a completely new way with its explanation of how gravity works. As a result, we understand the structure of the Universe, the physical relationship between stars and planets, and even galaxies, millions of light years apart, much more clearly than we did. Heisenberg, on the other hand, was fascinated not by the immensities of astronomy but by the unimaginably tiny world of the atom. In 1925 he announced his 'principle of indeterminacy' – a complex theory that stated, in effect, that the behaviour of the particles that made up the structure of the atom was chaotic and unpredictable. Einstein, far from appreciating Heisenberg's genius in recognising this, rejected the theory with words to the effect that 'God does not play dice with the Universe.' The irony of this story is that even Einstein's theory is so abtruse, so distant from our everyday understanding of reality, that most of us still do not understand it even though it was first published as long ago as 1905. The injustice of the story is that Heisenberg's ideas were not taught at Oxford University in England until after the Second World War.

And yet the fact remains that both Einstein and Heisenberg have come up with the best descriptions we have so far of the way the Universe works – on both the large and the small scale. But the resistance they met from other scientists was both powerful and irrational, for acceptance meant discard-ing many cherished – and apparently obvious – ideas. And to that extent the world we live in – dominated as it is by science and scientific theories – is neither tolerant nor dispassionate.

If scientists behave like this towards one another, their reception of notions which refuse to take the world at face value can easily be imagined, and this applies whether it is the possibility set out in this book that zombies are truly the 'living dead', or the proposal that memories may not live in the brain. Of all the unorthodox theories discussed in this book, perhaps the most exciting – and the most roundly abused – is Dr Rupert Sheldrake's 'hypothesis of formative causation': this somewhat daunting phrase covers a carefully constructed argument that reality has acquired certain *habits* that cause animals and plants to keep on forming in the ways that individual species do. And these habits are brought about by an as yet unidentified agency, which he calls 'morphogenetic fields' operating across space and time.

This seems unexceptional enough, but it flies in the face of current biological theory in two ways. In the first place, it rejects the assumption that living things are essentially if not exclusively material things. (Biologists insist, though without very good reason, that *all* the information about a plant or animal is contained in 'codes' – in other words, in the chemical structure of the acid known as DNA which is present in all living things and that is crucial in transmitting certain information from one generation to another.)

Secondly, Dr Sheldrake has no qualms about suggesting that we may not be able to perceive the actual nature of space and time.

For most biologists these two points are difficult enough to accept, but they perhaps reserve their greatest fury for the argument's *implied* point: that Charles Darwin was wrong. But as Dr Sheldrake argues, a belief in Darwin's ideas is exactly that: a matter of faith almost as much as belief in a religion is a matter of faith. Biologists cannot prove their assumptions are correct, even though they behave and work as if they were, and this makes them uncomfortable since scientists are popularly believed to deal only in provable certainties. In fact, it makes them look rather more like the dyed-in-the-wool men of religion who gave their hero Darwin such a difficult time when he first proposed his own theory! Scarcely surprising then, that the prestigious science journal *Nature* headlined a vitriolic (and badly reasoned) editorial assault on Dr Sheldrake, 'A book for burning?'

Scientists are usually able to defend themselves without resorting to hysteria however, and extremely effectively. It doesn't take a great deal of reasoned argument to shoot holes in the idea that the Earth is hollow – but then it doesn't take much by way of reasoned argument to propose that it is hollow in the first place. Since all the facts indicating that the Earth is solid are based on careful investigation and cautious calculation, while the argument that it is hollow has only the flimsiest of foundations, it is surprising that this idea has gained credence at all. No less extraordinary is the fact that otherwise reputable publishers have produced books purporting to offer evidence that the Earth is little more than a shell floating in space – 'evidence' that is more hilarious than persuasive.

One would have thought that this notion would have remained the exclusive property of cranks – the kind of people who still like to believe (contrary to all the evidence) that the Earth is flat. Yet the hollow Earth idea is surprisingly widespread. Why should this be so?

Unfortunately, as we have seen, the scientific community has a tendency to dismiss ideas that challenge its accepted beliefs. The result is that many people believe that *any* new theory will be rejected out of hand, whether it has real value or not. They then feel they have to examine revolutionary concepts themselves, and without the guiding hand and the hard evidence that science has to offer, they may accept some of them.

This situation creates a double misfortune, for not only are some people acting as narrowly towards scientists as they claim scientists act towards original thinkers, but their attitude is based on a complete misapprehension of the way science works. In the first place, science itself is no longer a single discipline but a huge network of related pursuits, and no single brain can possibly contain all the knowledge represented by that network. Two things follow this fact. One is that scientists are, quite properly, jealous of their professional standards, and recognise that only a small proportion of other scientists are really qualified to judge their work.

Consequently they do not take very kindly to the bright ideas of 'outsiders' – who may sometimes be other scientists. For a biologist to offer helpful advice to an astronomer is seen to be a little like a plumber taking it upon himself to interfere in the work of a brain surgeon. This caution, and the sheer scale of modern science, also means that science itself moves forward very slowly, like a gigantic intellectual tortoise. Scientists do not jump easily to conclusions, least of all when those conclusions are put up to them by people they regard as outsiders.

The closed nature of the scientific community does, however, have drawbacks. For example, if a field of enquiry is neglected by scientists for any reason, research in that area will be neglected or abandoned. Science, in this sense, is subject to fashion, since no scientist can really work in isolation from his fellows, no matter how dedicated he is or how good his ideas; he depends on the approval and criticism of other scientists.

From the outside, of course, it can seem very different indeed. Caution and a regard for professional ethics are necessary conditions of good research, and are admirable indeed. But they can all too easily appear to be the arrogance of an élite that is interested above all things in protecting its own interests. So, while there is every reason for scientists to approach new advances in knowledge with caution, it might also be sensible for them to treat the temptation to *reject* the unusual or the bizarre with a similar degree of inhibition.

The proposals of psychiatrist and space theorist Immanuel Velikovsky are a case in point. Subjected at first to merciless ostracism, Velikovsky has since been shown to have been right – even if not always for the same reasons – in certain of his assertions about the solar system, while his suggestion that the orthodox scholars' dating of certain events in ancient history was highly inaccurate is now being taken seriously.

Still, it's always possible to find someone who has been prepared to go one better than even the most glaring radical, and when it comes to revising our idea of history, no one has had a more athletic imagination than Comyns Beaumont, an exceedingly eccentric Englishman whose leaps and bounds of fantasy have the true flavour of the obsessed. More than anyone else in this volume, Comyns Beaumont thought the unthinkable, for the simple reason that only the highest order of crank could ever have contemplated such notions. His case reminds us that the scientists do have a point when they ask for new ideas to fit somewhere within an existing frame of reference. And he serves to remind us also that an acquaintance with the unorthodox can be amusing.

There is, of course, another species of unthinkable thought that haunts the mind of modern man: the advanced development of arcane technology – or the harnessing of much more sinister forces – for use in warfare. The democracies of the West already face an array of nuclear weaponry whose total destructive is unimaginably appalling. It is a grim enough thought that Soviet research may have exploited the little-known research of a neglected inventor, Nikola Tesla, who long made his home in the United States, in the hope of disrupting the West's defensive system. The possibility that, by massively investing in psychic research, Soviet influence could become overwhelming without a shot being fired, is enough to curl anyone's hair. And yet there is evidence that the existence of psi has long since been accepted by Soviet scientists (unlike their counterparts in the West) and that they are now concentrating on how to employ it. The prospect is made scarcely less appealing when one reflects that certain psychics in the West had become sufficiently adept in the early years of this century to be able to describe the structure of sub-atomic particles – a fact that has emerged only with the most advanced research in physics. (This extraordinary feat is described in this book by one of the physicists whose research confirmed the psychic findings.) Had the West seized the opportunities these achievements presented at the time, we might not have a threat of mental subversion facing us today.

This brings us back to where we started, with a sober reflection on how civilised the civilised world is – or isn't.

PETER BROOKESMITH

A penetrating vision

Modern physicists are probing ever deeper into the structure of matter, using costly and sophisticated technology. However, STEPHEN M. PHILLIPS asks whether some of their discoveries have been made before – by means of ancient Indian yoga techniques

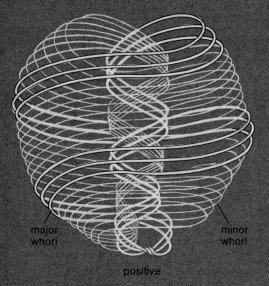

major whorl

positive

minor whorl

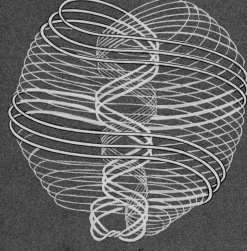

negative

Left: the two kinds of 'ultimate physical atom' seen clairvoyantly by Annie Besant and C.W. Leadbeater. The 'atoms' consisted of currents of energy forming spiral whorls. Colours constantly flashed out, changing according to which spiral was most active. The 'atoms' spun incessantly

THE TWO FIGURES WHO DOMINATED the Theosophical Society at the end of the 19th century, Annie Besant and Charles W. Leadbeater, began in 1895 a series of researches that was to last nearly 40 years. They were studying the ultimate structure of matter, using methods that orthodox science did not countenance: they were attempting to view atoms by extra-sensory perception. The vast amounts of information they produced seemed to bear no relationship to the findings of chemists and physicists during those four decades. Only in the 1980s were resemblances noticed between their descriptions and the modern theory of the structure of fundamental particles. It now seems possible that Besant and Leadbeater saw by occult means the 'quarks' that physicists postulate as the building blocks of matter.

The power of viewing the very small is one of the *siddhis*, or psychic faculties, that, according to Eastern tradition, can be cultivated by yoga meditation. In the ancient *Yoga sutras* the semi-legendary sage Patanjali lists the *siddhis*: one of them is the power to gain 'knowledge of the small, the hidden, or the distant by directing the light of a superphysical faculty'. This ability to acquire 'knowledge of the small' will be called 'micro-psi' in this chapter. Besant and Leadbeater claimed to have gained their micro-psi abilities under the tutelage of their Indian gurus.

To acquire knowledge paranormally that is confirmed by conventional science only

Below: Annie Besant with Charles Leadbeater. They divided their work while clairvoyantly viewing matter on the small scale, the highest magnifications being achieved by Mrs Besant. Their observations were in conflict with the science of their time

many years later is perhaps the most convincing type of ESP. In such cases there is no possibility that the psychic has access to normal sources of information. Whether or not the ESP was exercised under controlled laboratory conditions, it is impossible in principle to gain information by fraud or by means of the normal senses.

In 1895 Annie Besant and Charles Leadbeater published pictures of what they

The diagrams drawn from the descriptions provided by the two Theosophists Annie Besant and Charles Leadbeater give only a faint impression of the spectacle they witnessed. What they saw was confirmed by later clairvoyants using micro-psi (the faculty of viewing the very small) in the late 1950s. Initially a mist or haze of light appeared when they observed matter on the microscopic scale. With greater magnification the mist was resolved into myriad points of light, scintillating and moving chaotically. Some moved in regular orbits, forming the seven minor and three major

Window on the whorls

whorls of the 'atoms'. Some cascaded, like showers of meteors. The motions of the 'atoms' were confined to well-defined volumes of space, in any one of seven different geometric forms.

Each 'ultimate physical atom' was enclosed in a 'bubble', as if some transparent membrane surrounded it. The Theosophists spoke of space itself being pushed back by the dynamic activity of the matter in the 'atom'. This accorded with the complex theories of Theosophy, in which what we normally regard as a vacuum was only one of the seven states of matter.

claimed were hydrogen, nitrogen and oxygen atoms present in the air. According to their description a hydrogen atom was

> seen to consist of six small bodies, contained in an egg-like form . . . . It rotated with great rapidity on its own axis, vibrating at the same time, the internal bodies performing similar gyrations. The whole atom spins and quivers and has to be steadied before exact observation is possible. The six little bodies are arranged in two sets of three, forming two triangles that are not interchangeable.

Below left: the atom of hydrogen, according to Besant and Leadbeater. It was a transparent egg-shaped body containing smaller globes arranged in two interlinked triangles. Each one of the globes contained three of the 'ultimate physical atoms'

Below right: the seven geometrical forms of the micro-psi 'atoms'

But the 'six little bodies' were not the most basic units of matter. The psychics could magnify the images of them and found that each was composed of a globe enclosing three 'points of light'. When these in turn were highly magnified, they appeared as particles of definite size. Besant and Leadbeater called them 'ultimate physical atoms'.

Each of these 'ultimate' particles was seen to be made up of 10 convoluted spiral curves, or whorls, three of which (the 'major' whorls) appeared thicker or brighter than the other seven ('minor') whorls. The overall form of the whorls was that of a heart, with

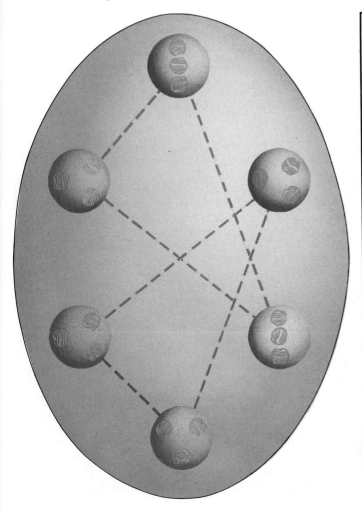

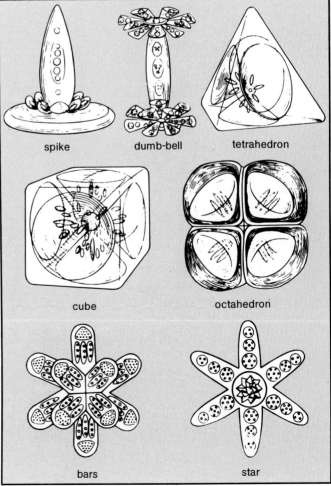

spike

dumb-bell

tetrahedron

cube

octahedron

bars

star

one end slightly concave and the other end pointed.

The Theosophists' description of matter differed greatly from the contemporary scientific notions of the atom. Two centuries earlier Sir Isaac Newton had conjectured that atoms were 'solid, massy, impenetrable'. In 1895 it was suspected that atoms in fact had a structure and that they were composed of smaller electrically charged particles. One of these was the electron, a hypothetical negatively charged particle much lighter than an atom. Electric currents were thought to consist of electrons in motion. In 1897 the electron's existence was demonstrated by the English physicist J. J. Thomson. Various models of the structure of the atom were then proposed. But the theory that finally won acceptance, as the result of the experimental and theoretical analyses of the physicists H. Geiger, E. Marsden and Lord Rutherford, was that of the 'nuclear' atom. They showed that the electrons in an atom orbited a tiny nucleus in which all the atom's positive charge and most of its mass were concentrated. When this was first demonstrated, from 1909 onwards, the electrons were supposed to move in well-defined orbits like those of the planets. They whirled around the nucleus millions of times per second, in a volume with a ten-millionth of the breadth of a pinhead. In the 1920s, with the advent of quantum mechanics, the electrons and their orbits came to be regarded as 'fuzzy' and ill-defined in position.

Ahead of the scientists

As each scientific picture of the atom was discarded and replaced by the next, Besant and Leadbeater continued to produce remarkably consistent descriptions of their 'micro-psi atoms', which at no time bore any resemblance to those of the scientists.

The two Theosophists observed that in certain elements – for example, the gases neon, argon, krypton and xenon and the metal platinum – the atoms were not all identical. This anticipated the scientific realisation that chemically indistinguishable variants of an element could exist, having atoms of different masses. These variants came to be called 'isotopes'.

One of the most important tools of orthodox chemistry is the periodic table. This is a classification of the elements in terms of their chemical properties and their atomic weights – the relative weights of their atoms, as determined chemically. The atomic weights of the elements increase as one reads across the table from left to right and down it from top to bottom. Chemical properties change systematically along each row of the table and down each column. Besant and Leadbeater found that the complex shape of the micro-psi 'atom' corresponded to the column of the periodic table in which that element lay.

When the two psychics began their

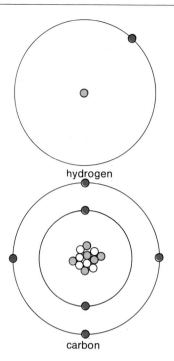

hydrogen

carbon

Above: in the scientific picture, the nucleus of hydrogen is a single positively charged particle, the proton. The nuclei of heavier atoms, such as carbon, consist of protons and neutral particles called neutrons. Negatively charged electrons circle the nucleus

Below: isotopes of an element such as neon have equal numbers of protons, but different numbers of neutrons

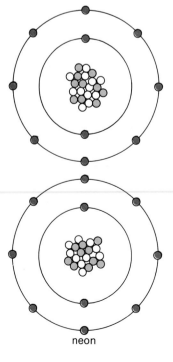

neon

research, between 60 and 70 elements were known (of the 90 or so that occur in nature) and there were many gaps in the periodic table. Besant and Leadbeater described a number of types of micro-psi 'atom' that corresponded, they believed, to gaps in the periodic table. The existence of these elements, and many of their properties, could be predicted by conventional science, but they had not yet been observed.

The two psychics discovered that the number of 'ultimate' particles in the micro-psi 'atoms' was very nearly equal to 18 times the atomic weight of the corresponding element. (The atomic weight of an element is the average weight of the atoms of its various isotopes. Scientists at that time took their unit to be the weight of the hydrogen atom.) Thus hydrogen, with the atomic weight 1, had 18 'ultimate' particles; carbon, with an atomic weight of 12, had 216.

The 'atoms' that the two psychics described were sometimes seen to be combined into larger units, just as the corresponding chemical atoms combined into larger groupings, called molecules. The micro-psi 'atoms' were combined in the same numbers as the atoms known to science. But, in total violation of all that was known to chemistry, micro-psi 'atoms' were observed to be broken up and their constituent particles mixed with those of other atoms. Sceptics felt that this discredited Besant and Leadbeater's claims, since chemical atoms do not split up and mix with each other wholesale when they combine, though they share or transfer some outer electrons.

Other problems emerged. For example, Leadbeater described the micro-psi molecule of the compound benzene as being octahedral – that is, as having the overall shape of an eight-faced solid. But chemists already knew that the chemical molecule of benzene was flat and hexagonal. And the psychics described micro-psi 'atoms' of several supposed elements for which there was no room whatever in the periodic table.

Such problems as these add up to overwhelming evidence against the two Theosophists' interpretation of the micro-psi 'atoms' as being the atoms studied by the chemist. Neither could they have been the nuclei of atoms, which do not split up in chemical reactions. What, then, were they? If they were merely hallucinations, why should the number of 'ultimate' constituents, of which there could be several thousand, always have been 18 times the correct atomic weight? Why should the forms described by Besant and Leadbeater have correlated with the position of the element in the periodic table? How could the two workers have 'guessed' that some atoms exist in different forms five years before scientists suspected the existence of isotopes?

The hunting of the quark

In the early 20th century two leading Theosophists claimed to have probed the atom by clairvoyant vision. Scientists can now identify a number of parallels between their account and modern scientific theories

TODAY, WHEN PEOPLE OSTENSIBLY bend spoons without touching them and leather rings link themselves together of their own accord on film, the claims of English mystics Annie Besant and Charles W. Leadbeater that they observed fundamental particles by psychic means seem less fantastic than they did in the early 1900s. But both prejudice and well-founded criticism have until recently made the two Theosophists' claims seem false and absurd to most scientists. Chemists as distinguished as E. Lester Smith, co-discoverer of vitamin B_{12}, pointed out the discrepancies between the descriptions of micro-psi 'atoms' and the current

quantity of hydrogen that exists under ordinary conditions. This much was well-known even when Besant and Leadbeater began their work. Then it was discovered that each hydrogen atom consisted of a single proton – a positively charged particle – around which an electron – a negatively charged particle, much lighter than a proton – revolved in an orbit.

In 1964 the quark theory was proposed by the American physicists Murray Gell-Mann and George Zweig, working independently. They proposed that protons and neutrons – neutral particles of approximately the same mass as protons, occurring in all nuclei except the simplest, that of hydrogen – are made up of three fundamental particles called 'quarks'. So too are other relatively heavy particles studied by physicists. Several scientists, including this author, have gone further and have suggested the existence of

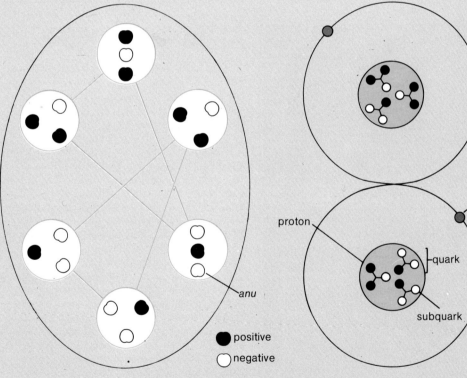

positive
negative

proton
electron
quark
subquark
anu

The structure (far left) believed by Annie Besant and C.W. Leadbeater to be the hydrogen atom may have been derived from a *pair* of atoms, linked to form a molecule (left). The fundamental *anu* would then correspond to hypothetical particles called subquarks. Three subquarks make up a quark, while the *anu* likewise occurred in triplets. Furthermore, subquarks come in two varieties, just as the *anu* did. Three quarks make up each atom's central proton, corresponding to each of the two triangular arrays 'seen' by the psychics. It seems that the hydrogen atoms must have been disrupted and intermixed when observed psychically; furthermore, the two electrons did not appear

knowledge of chemical atoms. Sympathetic scientists lost any hope of reconciling Besant and Leadbeater's work with orthodox science.

What, then, were Besant and Leadbeater 'seeing'? In the 1970s the present author pointed out a solution to this problem. The two psychics' description of what they believed to be the hydrogen atom provides the vital clue to the puzzle.

In its normal state hydrogen does not consist of single atoms. It consists of pairs of atoms, tightly bound together. This pair is the 'molecule' of hydrogen – the smallest

'subquarks' of which the quarks are supposedly composed.

Compare this picture with the micro-psi 'atom' of hydrogen, as described by Besant and Leadbeater. It consists of two intersecting triangular arrays, each consisting of three bodies. Each of these bodies in turn consists of three particles that the psychics named 'ultimate physical atoms'. They also referred to them as *anu*, a Sanskrit word, meaning 'atoms'. Can we identify these with subquarks? If we can, then three of them form a quark, which we can identify with the body lying at each corner of one of the triangular

Murray Gell-Mann shared a Nobel prize for proposing the theory that certain types of fundamental particle are composed of yet smaller 'quarks'

arrays. And each triangular array is a proton. The micro-psi hydrogen 'atom' is actually a structure derived from the hydrogen *molecule* with its two protons.

This interpretation explains why micropsi 'atoms' of hydrogen were never observed in pairs, as would be expected if they were chemical atoms. But as observed by the two Theosophists, the protons appeared to be much closer together than we now know them to be in the hydrogen molecule – 100,000 times closer, in fact. To explain this it is necessary to suppose that the two atomic nuclei disintegrated and their constituent quarks recombined, at least for the period during which they were being observed by micro-psi.

The atomic weight of an element is defined as the weight of one of its atoms relative to the weight of one atom of hydrogen. Thus carbon, for example, has an atomic weight of 12 because its atom is 12 times as heavy as hydrogen's. But since a hydrogen atom weighs almost the same as a proton, which in turn is very close in weight to a neutron, the atomic weight of an element is almost exactly equal to the number of protons and neutrons in its atomic nucleus. Different isotopes of an element have different numbers of neutrons in the atomic nucleus, and their atomic weights differ accordingly. Furthermore, on the theory we are here considering, the number of subquarks very nearly equals nine times the atomic weight (because there are three subquarks per quark, and three quarks per proton or neutron).

The number of subquarks in any *pair* of nuclei of a given element is therefore close to 18 times the atomic weight of that element. And Besant and Leadbeater found that the number of *anu* in each micro-psi 'atom' was about 18 times the atomic weight of that element. So it seems that the two researchers were observing pairs of nuclei that had disintegrated and recombined, and they were succeeding in distinguishing the subquarks that made them up.

Usually the number of *anu* in an atom was not exactly equal to 18 times the atomic weight of the element. Now, Besant and Leadbeater had to estimate the number of *anu* in the more complex micro-psi atoms by

In his own image

Besant and Leadbeater related the structure of the *anu* to the ancient Jewish mystical doctrine of the Tree of Life. This is a kind of chart of reality, including the material Universe and its microcosm, the human body. The Tree is based on 10 *sephiroth* ('emanations') – the 10 stages in which God manifested himself in creation. Masculine qualities are placed on the right, feminine ones on the left. They are combined and reconciled in the central *sephiroth*. The highest is Kether (Crown, or godhead), giving rise to Chokmah (divine Wisdom) and Binah (divine Intelligence). A gulf separates this 'supernal triad' from the lower *sephiroth*. Chesed (Mercy) is a constructive, loving principle, contrasted with Geburah (Severity), which is associated with destruction and war. These two are united in Tiphereth (Beauty), representing the life force and symbolised by the Sun and by the heart. Next come Netzagh (Victory), representing instinct, the passions and forces of attraction, and Hod (Glory), standing for imagination, and also for reason, which is viewed as a negative quality. Yesod (Foundation) is linked with growth and decay, the Moon – which links the Sun and the Earth – and the genitals. Malkuth (Kingdom) is matter, the Earth, the body. To Besant and Leadbeater the three major whorls of the *anu* corresponded to the supernal triad and the remainder to the lower seven *sephiroth*.

counting them in individual 'spikes' or 'bars' and then multiplying by the number of such spikes or bars in the whole 'atom'. For example, the micro-psi 'atom' of one of the isotopes of neon is star-shaped. It consists of a central globe containing 120 *anu*, and six arms, each containing 46 *anu*. Besant and Leadbeater apparently counted 47 *anu* in one of these arms and thus overestimated the total number in the 'atom' by six. Almost all of the discrepancies in the numbers of *anu* reported by the psychics can be accounted for as the results of miscounting by one or two in one part of the structure they were observing – a structure that was complex and shifting, and could contain thousands of *anu*, so that such small errors are only to be expected.

Besant and Leadbeater commented on the difficulties they had in stopping the

isotopes of a single element.

Further confirmation of the objective character of the Theosophists' observations is provided by their descriptions of the forces binding the *anu* together. They support the 'string model', which accounts for the forces between quarks.

This theory was developed because free quarks have never been detected, despite extensive searches over the years. Physicists concluded that these particles cannot escape from one another. The string model explains this by regarding quarks as resembling the ends of a piece of string. If the model is correct, then we can no more hope to find a free quark than we can hope to find a piece of string with a single end. The quark is regarded as a magnetic 'monopole' – a single source of magnetic field. The magnetic field can be visualised in terms of 'lines of force',

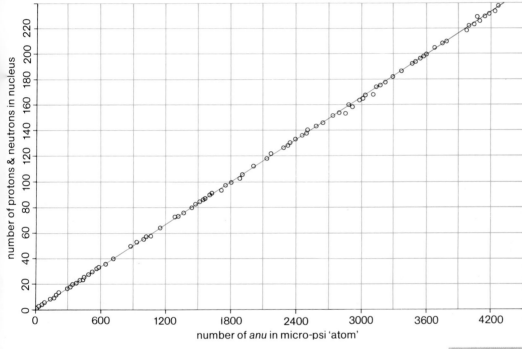

motion of the constituent particles by psychokinesis. Leadbeater once said:

> The molecule is spinning. You have to hold it still and then you have to be careful that you do not spoil its shape. I am always afraid of disturbing the things because I must stop their motion in order to give an idea of them.

What of the 'atoms' described by Besant and Leadbeater for which there are no places in the periodic table? These could have been formed from the nuclei of two different elements, with micro-psi 'atoms' of the same shape. The numbers of *anu* support this conjecture. One such anomalous object contained 2646 *anu*, equivalent to an atomic weight of 147. This is the average of 102 and 192, the atomic weights of the most common isotopes of ruthenium and osmium, which had micro-psi 'atoms' of the same shape. Further 'impossible' structures could be formed by the combination of different

Above: a graph of the number of particles in each atomic nucleus – a number approximately equal to the atomic weight – against the number of *anu* seen in the atom by Besant and Leadbeater. If there were exactly 18 *anu* for each particle, all the points would lie on the red line. Small departures from the line could be due to small, plausible errors in counting by the psychics. The graph is impressive evidence that they were observing something objectively real

Below: the collaborator and amanuensis of Besant and Leadbeater, C. Jinarajadasa, who took down their descriptions as they made their psychic observations

or field lines, like those traced out by iron filings shaken onto a piece of paper held over a bar magnet. The field lines from a quark form a narrow tube or string – the physicist thinks of the lines as being squeezed together by surrounding space. A quark and its corresponding antiquark (which is its antimatter equivalent or mirror particle at the end of a string form one of a number of short-lived particles called mesons. Three quarks lying at the ends of a Y-shaped string form other types of particles, including protons and neutrons. If a string breaks, new quarks appear at the severed ends.

If quarks are regarded as themselves composite particles, then they consist of triplets of subquarks, and it is these that lie at the ends of Y-shaped strings.

Compare this picture with the diagrams of pairs and triplets of *anu* observed by Besant

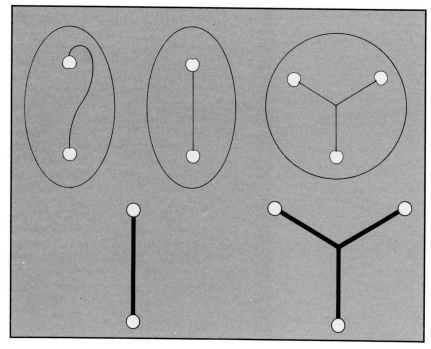

and Leadbeater. Some pairs were joined by single 'lines of force'. Sometimes three lines of force formed a Y-shaped configuration, each line ending on an *anu*. Such diagrams are, essentially, identical to depictions of subatomic particles appearing in the scientific journals of today.

Annie Besant took responsibility for observing how the *anu* were bound together, whereas Leadbeater was concerned with the larger-scale structures, requiring less magnification. Besant depicted many string configurations, in addition to the single strings and Y-shaped strings. Together they add up to further evidence that the *anu* were single magnetic poles bound by string-like lines of force. Her observations give support from an unexpected direction to a modern scientific theory of the strong forces acting between fundamental particles.

The two Theosophists were assisted in their work by their friend C. Jinarajadasa

Above: structures (above) described by Besant and Leadbeater. They strikingly resemble modern 'string model' theories (below) in which quarks (or subquarks) are the ends of 'strings' of magnetic lines of force

Top: Annie Besant and Charles Leadbeater conducted their research into the constitution of matter over four decades, while also controlling the affairs of the Theosophical Society. Another of their shared concerns was a belief in reincarnation

who wrote down their descriptions as they dictated them. At the end of the third edition of *Occult chemistry*, he remarked:

> With the information revealed in *Occult chemistry*, a great expansion of our knowledge of Chemistry lies in front of us. It is just because this expansion is inevitable, that our clairvoyant investigators have toiled patiently for thirty years. They have claimed no recognition from chemists and physicists, because truth accepted or rejected is truth still, and any fact of nature seen and stated clearly will sooner or later be woven into the whole fabric of truth. The fact that this generation of scientists hardly knows anything at all of an extraordinary work of research extending for thirty years matters little, when we contemplate the long vistas of scientific investigation which the imagination sees awaiting mankind.

Today the 'extraordinary piece of research' by Besant and Leadbeater has at last shown its intrinsic scientific merit by revealing a remarkably high degree of consistency with ideas and well-established facts of nuclear and particle physics. Without knowing what they were observing, they described the subatomic world 70 years ago in a way that agrees with important areas of modern research. Scientists and lay people alike may find their claims difficult to believe. But they cannot dismiss the Theosophists' claims as fraudulent because their work was completed many years before pertinent scientific knowledge and theories became available to make a hoax possible even in principle. Nor can they honestly reject these claims as unsupported by scientific thought, for the very opposite is true. How, therefore, can one account for Besant and Leadbeater's remarkable anticipations of modern physics except by admitting that they did indeed observe the microphysical world by means of extra-sensory perception?

Creatures of habit

Do we inherit knowledge from past generations? Experiments suggest we may have access to a kind of 'pooled memory' – the collective knowledge of our entire species. RUPERT SHELDRAKE shows how the facts support his revolutionary theory of heredity

WHEN RABBITS BREED, they produce more rabbits; goldfish produce goldfish; and seeds from cabbage plants grow into cabbages. Like begets like. The general characteristics of the species are produced again and again, generation after generation; so are particular features of the race or variety, and even individual features that enable us to pick out family resemblances.

These facts are so familiar that we tend to take them for granted. But the more that is found out about the intricate processes by which embryos develop and grow, the more amazing this inheritance of shape and structure becomes. Even more astonishing is the inheritance of instinct. Young spiders, for example, spin their webs without having to learn from other spiders how to do it, or what the webs are for. Among the birds, cuckoos provide a particularly striking example: the young are hatched and reared by foster parents of other species, and never see their true parents or, indeed, any other cuckoos, for the first few weeks of their lives. Towards the end of the summer, adult European cuckoos migrate to their winter habitat in southern Africa. About a month later, the young cuckoos congregate together and then they also migrate to the appropriate region of Africa, where they join the older generation. They instinctively know that they should migrate, and when to do so; they instinctively recognise other young cuckoos and congregate together; and they instinctively know in which direction to fly and where their destination is.

How can these phenomena of heredity be explained? The most obvious fact to start with is that all animals and plants develop from living cells derived from their parents. In sexual reproduction these are the egg and sperm cells, and in vegetative reproduction detached parts of the parent organism, as in the propagation of plants by cuttings. These cells have a complex microscopic structure, and in the nucleus of each one are long thread-like chromosomes, which contain the chemical DNA (deoxyribonucleic acid).

It is well known that one of the major triumphs of modern biology has been to show that hereditary differences between organisms depend on differences in specific parts of their chromosomes, called genes, and that the DNA of different genes has a definite and characteristic structure.

DNA comes in pairs of long strands wrapped around each other in a spiral – the famous double helix. On these strands are four different kinds of chemical, usually represented by the letters A, G, T and C – adenine, guanine, thymine and cytosine – and these can be arranged in different sequences to spell out different chemical 'words'. These sequences of 'words' can be translated into sequences of relatively simple chemicals, amino acids, which are strung together to make up protein molecules. Proteins are the complicated chemicals that make up much of the protoplasm and that, as enzymes, catalyse the chemical reactions within cells.

These discoveries have often been described, and there is no need to go into more detail here. The important question is: can these chemicals *by themselves* explain the problem of heredity? Can we in fact account for the shape of a flower or the instincts of an insect in terms of the chemicals it contains?

The answer is that we cannot. Biologists are agreed on this point. But whereas most of them assume that the failure so far is due to the fact that living organisms are extremely

The intricate pattern of a spider's web. Young spiders know instinctively how to weave webs – without having to learn the skill from other spiders. How are such instincts inherited?

complex and that not enough is yet known about their chemical details, some – including this author – are convinced that we can never understand living organisms in terms of chemistry alone. Other, still mysterious, factors are involved in life, and play a major part in the inheritance of form and instinct.

Even orthodox biologists admit the existence of a mysterious non-chemical factor in heredity. They give it the impressive-sounding name: the 'genetic programme'. Thus it would be said, for example, that the shape of a daffodil or the instincts of a dragonfly are 'genetically programmed'. But what exactly is a genetic programme?

It is not like a computer program, because this is put into a computer by a conscious intelligent being, the computer programmer – and materialistically minded biologists deny that living organisms have been put together by a conscious programmer or designer.

Is the genetic programme the same thing as the chemical structure of the DNA? This cannot be the explanation either, because all cells of the body contain identical copies of DNA, and yet they develop differently. Consider your arms and your legs. The DNA in them is the same, but they have different forms. So something *else* must have been responsible for shaping them as they developed in the embryo.

The conventional explanation is that this shaping must be due to complicated chemical and physical interactions that are not yet understood. But what gives rise to the correct pattern of interactions? This is the problem that remains unsolved, and to say that it must be due to a genetic programme does not in fact provide any explanation at all; it merely creates an illusion of understanding. Similarly, to say that a spider's nervous system is genetically programmed to give the right web-spinning behaviour only restates the problem in different words.

Through detailed study of embryos, a number of influential embryologists have come to the conclusion that the developing limbs and organs are shaped by what they call *morphogenetic fields*. This term is not as

Above: a reed warbler feeds a young cuckoo in its nest. Cuckoos are hatched and reared by birds of other species and, for the first few weeks of their lives, they see no other cuckoos. But, at the end of the summer, the young cuckoos, taught by no one, join up into groups to make the long flight to their winter habitat in southern Africa. They know instinctively when to congregate, how to recognise other cuckoos – and how to navigate on the long journey that none of them has attempted before. How can this complex behaviour be explained?

The genetic blueprint

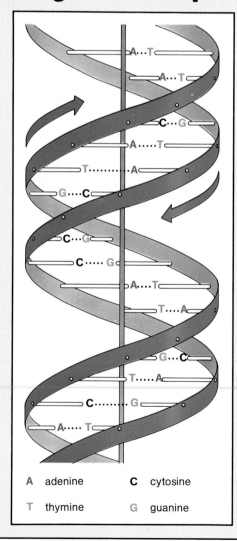

A	adenine	C	cytosine
T	thymine	G	guanine

The discovery by James Watson and Francis Crick in 1953 of the beautiful double helix structure of DNA (left) is famous as one of the great breakthroughs of modern science. But the function of this substance is less well-known.

DNA – deoxyribonucleic acid – is essentially the carrier of genetic information. Found in the reproductive cells of all living things are long paired strands called chromosomes, which are the carriers of the genes. There is a fixed number of pairs of chromosomes for each species; the number for Man is 23.

Genes are made up of proteins and DNA. Scientists had believed that the proteins were the genetic material, but in the early 1950s DNA – a substance that had been isolated in cells as early as 1869 – was recognised as the carrier of encoded genetic information.

It remained to break the code. The first decisive step forward came with Crick and Watson's discovery of 1953. They found that DNA consists of chains of sugar and phosphate, twisted round each other and carrying four different kinds of molecule – adenine, guanine, thymine and cytosine – which can be arranged to form various instructions. These control the selection and arrangement of amino acids, which are used to manufacture proteins. Thus DNA controls every aspect of the development of the body.

But one puzzle remains: all the cells of the body contain identical copies of DNA, and yet they develop differently. What controls this development? Orthodox science has, as yet, no answer.

daunting as it sounds at first: it means fields that give rise to form, or 'form-fields' (the word 'morphogenetic' comes from the Greek *morphe* which means form, and *genesis* which means coming-into-being). These fields can be thought of by analogy with magnetic fields, which have a shape even though they are invisible. (The shape of the field of a magnet can be revealed by the patterns taken up by iron filings scattered around it.) The form-fields mould the developing cells and tissues. Thus, in the embryo, a developing arm is moulded by an 'arm-shaping' morphogenetic field and a developing leg by a 'leg-shaping' field.

But what are these fields, and where do they come from? For over 50 years, their nature and even their existence has remained obscure. However, these fields are just as real as the magnetic and gravitational fields of physics, but they are a new kind of field with very remarkable properties. Like the known fields of physics, they connect similar things together across space, with seemingly nothing in between – but in addition they

Below: a human foetus at various stages of development. At 28 days (top left) it is no more than a small blob of tissue nestled in the womb lining; at 33 days (top right) the limbs are just beginning to appear; at 49 days (bottom left) the features are recognisably human – and finally, after 340 days in the womb, the baby is fully developed (bottom right). *Something* has supervised the highly specialised development of the various parts of the baby's body – and yet, since the DNA in each of its cells is identical to that of its original single cell, this 'something' must be different from the genetic information encoded in the DNA. Its nature is, as yet, unknown

connect things together across *time*, so that creatures can learn from the experience of previous members of the same species even when there is no direct contact.

The idea is that the morphogenetic fields that shape a growing animal or plant are derived from the forms of previous organisms of the same species. The embryo as it were 'tunes in' to the form of past members of the species. The process by which this happens is called *morphic resonance*. Similarly, the fields that organise the activities of an animal's nervous system are derived from past animals of the same kind; in their instinctive behaviour animals draw on a sort of 'memory bank' or 'pooled memory' of their species.

Learning new tricks
This hypothesis, which is known as the hypothesis of formative causation, leads to a range of surprising predictions that provide ways of testing it experimentally. For instance, if a number of animals, say rats, learn a new trick that rats have never performed before, then other rats of the same kind all over the world should be able to learn the same trick more easily, even in the absence of any known kind of connection or communication. The larger the number of rats that learn it, the easier it should become for subsequent rats everywhere else.

Remarkably enough, there is already evidence that this phenomenon actually occurs. In 1920, the psychologist William McDougall began at Harvard University a series of experiments designed to find out if animals were able to inherit abilities acquired by their parents. He put white rats, one at a time, in a tank of water from which they could escape only by swimming to one of two gangways and climbing up it. One gangway was brightly lit, the other was not. If the rats left by the illuminated gangway, they received an electric shock. McDougall recorded how many trials the rats took to learn always to escape by the other one.

The first generation of rats received an average of over 160 shocks each before learning to avoid the illuminated gangway. But the second generation, bred from these experienced parents, learned quicker, and the next generation quicker still. This improvement continued until after 30 generations the rats were making an average of only 20 errors each.

McDougall believed that his results provided good evidence for the inheritance of acquired characteristics. This conclusion was extremely controversial. It flew in the face of the orthodox theory of inheritance, based on Mendelian genetics, which denies that any such thing can happen. His experiments were subjected to critical scrutiny by some of the leading biologists of the time. But they were able to find little wrong with the experimental procedure, and fell back on the criticism that McDougall must have been

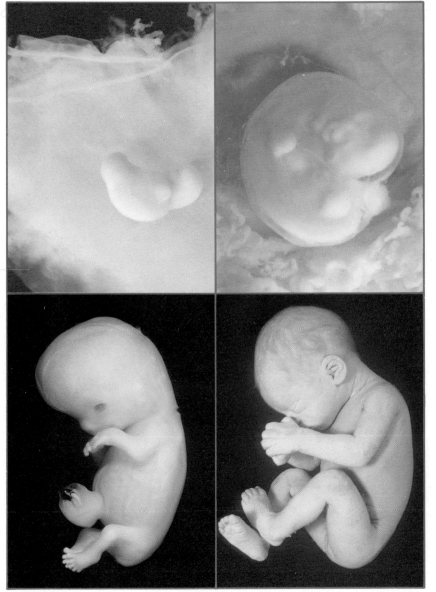

breeding from the more intelligent rats in each generation, in spite of the fact that he chose the parents at random.

He replied by starting a new experiment in which he selected only the most *stupid* rats in each generation as parents of the next. According to conventional genetics, subsequent generations should have got slower and slower at learning. But in fact the reverse occurred, and after 22 generations the rats were learning 10 times faster than the first generation of stupid ancestors.

These results had such revolutionary implications that other scientists hastened to try to repeat them. Dr F.A.E. Crew in Edinburgh, and Prof. W.E. Agar and his colleagues in Melbourne, Australia, constructed tanks of similar design, using white rats of the same breed. But for reasons that no one was able to explain, from the very first generation their rats picked up what was going on *much quicker* than the early generations of McDougall's. So striking was this effect that some of the first rats Crew tested 'learned' to escape by the unlit gangway straight away, without making a single error.

Agar and his group studied not only the change in the rate of learning of successive generations of rats descended from trained parents, as McDougall had done, but also that of a parallel line of rats bred from untrained parents. In this control line, some of the rats were tested in the water tank and then discarded and replaced by others that had not been tested, who then became the parents of the next generation of control

Above: chromosomes picked out clearly by a special dye in the salivary glands of the fruit-fly *Drosophila*, here magnified 120 times. Found in paired strands in the nuclei of sex cells, chromosomes bear the genes that are the carriers of hereditary information. When two creatures reproduce sexually, the offspring receives one set of chromosomes from each of its parents

animals as the experiment continued.

In experiments that lasted 25 years, these Australian workers observed that successive generations of rats in the trained lines tended to learn quicker and quicker, just as McDougall had found. *But so did the rats in the control line.*

The fact that the same improvement occurred in rats descended both from trained and from untrained ancestors showed that it could not be due to the passing on of specifically modified genes from parents to their offspring. Therefore McDougall's conclusion was refuted. With the publication of the final paper by Agar's group in 1954, the last surviving piece of evidence for the inheritance of acquired characteristics seemed to have been disposed of. Nevertheless, McDougall's remarkable results were confirmed, and to this day they have remained unexplained in terms of orthodox science. But to regard them merely as a refutation of the inheritance of acquired characteristics is to overlook what is potentially a far more revolutionary discovery. For Agar's and McDougall's results fit in extremely well with the hypothesis of formative causation.

In relation to human beings, this hypothesis suggests that, on average, it should be getting easier and easier for people to learn to ride bicycles, or to type, or to swim, just because more and more people have already learned to do these things. Is this in fact the case? Unfortunately data are hard to come by, although anecdotal evidence suggests that such improvements have in fact occurred. But even if this is so, changes in the average speed of learning are difficult to

interpret because other relevant factors also change with time, like machine design, teaching methods, and motivation.

The idea of morphic resonance is perhaps easier to grasp with the help of an analogy. Imagine an intelligent and curious person who knows nothing about electricity or electromagnetic radiation. He is shown a television set for the first time. He might at first suppose that the set actually contained little people, whose images he saw on the screen. But when he looked inside and found only wires, condensers, transistors, and so on, he might adopt the more sophisticated theory

readily the more often they have been crystallised before.

New chemicals synthesised for the first time are usually difficult to crystallise, and they do in fact tend to form crystals more readily as time goes on. The conventional explanation is that tiny fragments of previous crystals get carried from laboratory to laboratory on the clothing of scientists, or that crystal 'seeds' travel round the world as microscopic dust particles in the atmosphere. But, as Dr Sheldrake points out, it would be easy enough to eliminate these possibilities in a sealed laboratory.

○ sodium

● chlorine

As clear as crystal?

It is in the field of chemistry that the most unambiguous tests of the hypothesis of formative causation should be possible. Dr Sheldrake's hypothesis predicts, for example, that the complex patterns in which molecules arrange themselves (like the perfect cube formed by sodium chloride, or common salt, above and right) should be influenced by the patterns taken up by previous crystals of the same substance. Substances should crystallise the more

Left: the pattern produced by a bar magnet when iron filings are scattered around it. The magnetic field that gives rise to the pattern is always there (see inset) – but it is usually invisible. Some leading embryologists believe that the shape of living things is formed by a *morphogenetic field* – a field that, although usually invisible like the magnetic field, can nevertheless mould the developing cells and tissues of an organism

that the screen images somehow arose from complicated interactions among the components of the set. This hypothesis would seem particularly plausible when he found that the images became distorted or disappeared completely when components were removed, and that the images were restored to normal when these components were put back in their proper places.

If the suggestion were put to him that the images also depended on invisible influences entering the set from far away, he might reject it on the grounds that it was unnecessary and obscurantist. His opinion that nothing came into the set from outside would be reinforced by the discovery that the set weighed the same switched on and switched off. While admitting that he could not explain in detail how the images were produced from complicated interactions within the set, and nothing more, he might well claim that such an explanation was possible in principle, and that it would in fact eventually be achieved after a great deal of further research.

This point of view may resemble the conventional approach to biology. By contrast, in terms of this analogy the hypothesis of formative causation does not involve a

denial of the importance of the wires and transistors (corresponding to DNA, protein molecules, and so on); but it recognises in addition the role of influences transmitted from outside the system, the 'transmitters' being past organisms of the same species. Genetic changes can affect the inheritance of form or instinct by altering the 'tuning', or by introducing distortions into the 'reception'. But genetic factors cannot by themselves fully account for the inheritance of form and instinct, any more than the particular pictures on the screen of a television set can be explained in terms of its wiring diagram alone.

The hypothesis of formative causation leads to an interpretation of heredity in terms of the repetition of forms and patterns of behaviour that have occurred in the past. But it cannot in itself lead to an understanding of how these forms and patterns originated in the first place. This question can be answered in several different ways – but all of them seem to be equally compatible with the suggested means of repetition.

Where did Darwin go wrong?

Does the neo-Darwinian theory of natural selection really conflict with the biblical account of creation? Can it account for the astonishing variety of living things?

THE THEORY OF EVOLUTION, in its most general terms, states that new species of plants and animals are descended from species that existed before them. This is what used to be called the theory of descent, or transformism. It was widely known and discussed for two generations before Charles Darwin published his *Origin of species* in 1859; indeed, one version was proposed by his grandfather, Erasmus Darwin, in 1794; another was put forward by the French scientist Jean Baptiste Lamarck in 1809.

Darwin's theory conflicted with the view of the leading philosophers of the ancient world, most notably Aristotle, that species were eternally fixed and unchangeable. In the light of this classical philosophy, the biblical account of creation in the book of Genesis was interpreted to mean that God directly created all the different species of plants and animals, and that they remained unchanged thereafter.

The theory of evolution by descent was opposed throughout the 19th century – and is still opposed – by biblical fundamentalists. However, among scientists it has been widely accepted for decades, and is generally taken for granted. But to accept that species have evolved from other species – what is often referred to as the 'fact' of evolution – raises

The 19th century saw a violent clash between two conflicting views of evolution. Christian doctrine stated that the world and all that lives upon it was created by God in six days – as shown in this painting by Tintoretto (above). Charles Darwin (right) introduced a revolutionary new theory in his *Origin of species*, published in 1859, in which he suggested that evolution proceeds by the brutal process of natural selection

the questions of why species should have changed, and of how they do so. This is an area of much controversy within science.

In his famous book, whose full title was *On the origin of species by means of natural selection, or the preservation of favoured races in the struggle for life*, Charles Darwin put forward a particular theory of the way in which evolution occurred. In doing so, he made the notion of evolution by descent much more credible than it had been before, because he was able to suggest a plausible mechanism – natural selection – for the transformation of species. Thenceforth the general theory of evolution by descent and Darwin's theory of natural selection became closely associated with each other. However, it is important to realise that it is possible to accept the idea of evolution without accepting Darwin's explanation of it.

Although the arguments for evolution are

well-known, it seems worth reminding ourselves of them. The first depends on the fossil record, in which the remains of vast numbers of animals and plants are preserved, often in layers that indicate the sequence in which they were laid down. These fossils show that many of the different kinds of animals and plants that once existed on the Earth have become extinct. The best-known are the giant reptiles, such as the dinosaurs, which died out about 70 million years ago.

Since in many cases new types of organism resemble ones that existed before them, it is reasonable to suppose that they were descended from pre-existing species. For example, the birds and mammals appeared long after the reptiles had become established, and share many anatomical features, such as having two pairs of limbs with five digits at the end, which in spite of their different modifications in the wings of birds, fingers of men, and flippers of whales, show a common underlying pattern.

The second reason for thinking that evolution occurs is provided by the many different breeds and varieties of domesticated animals and plants. Think for example, of the differences between dogs such as greyhounds and Pekinese. The fact that these have been produced by selective breeding from similar ancestral stock shows that the form of the species is not rigidly fixed, but can change with time.

Thirdly, the geographical distribution of certain species of plants and animals suggests that they have evolved by descent. An example that greatly impressed Darwin was that of the finches native to the Galapagos Islands, off the coast of South America. Distinct species, adapted to different methods of feeding, occur on these islands within short distances, while on the mainland there are closely related finches. The simplest explanation of these facts is that a few finches migrated from the mainland to the islands, and that some of their descendants evolved into new species adapted to the local conditions. Many other similar examples have been described.

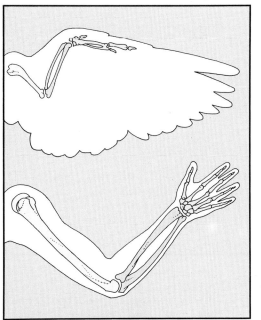

Left: the wing of a bird (top) and the arm of a human being (bottom) which, although very different in appearance, have similar structures. This fact is strong evidence for evolution, suggesting that birds and men have a common ancestor from which the wing and arm structure is evolved. The leading philosophers of the ancient world had believed that species were eternally fixed and unchangeable

Above: a Staffordshire bull terrier. When bull-baiting died out in England, around 1835, dog-fighting became popular, and the breed of Staffordshire bull terrier was created by crossing bulldogs and terriers. It is the result of a particularly ruthless form of selection: dogs that were not good fighters were simply drowned

Lastly, the fact that animals and plants can be grouped together in hierarchical systems of classification supports the notion of descent. For instance, the human species is grouped with the primates, together with monkeys and apes; the primates are grouped with other mammals; and the mammals with other vertebrates. The similarities within each group are most easily explained in terms of descent from common ancestors; the bigger the grouping, the more remote the ancestral links.

The only alternative to the evolutionary interpretation of the evidence is to suppose that species were specially created from non-living matter at frequent intervals over a long period of time, in such a way that new species resembled species that had been created before them, and in the same geographical areas.

This seems extremely implausible, but some people feel bound to adopt this theory in an attempt to harmonise the factual evidence with one particular interpretation of the accounts of creation in the book of

Left: a model skeleton of the dinosaur *Tyrannosaurus rex*. Dinosaurs died out about 70 million years ago, but their fossil remains survive, providing powerful support for the theory of evolution

Learning from experience

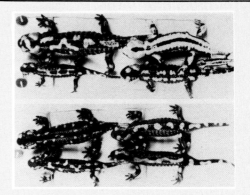

Can acquired characteristics be inherited? The neo-Darwinian answer is a categorical no – but there exists experimental evidence that suggests otherwise.

Between 1903 and 1908 a brilliant young Austrian biologist named Paul Kammerer conducted a series of very interesting experiments with spotted salamanders, *Salamandra maculosa*. These newt-like creatures have yellow spots on a black ground; and, like the chameleon, they will change colour according to their background.

Kammerer raised two groups of salamanders, one on yellow sand (top panel, left), the other on black sand (bottom panel, left). Sure enough, the salamanders changed colour.

His next step was to breed from these salamanders, to see whether their adapted colouring was passed on to the next generation. And, astoundingly, it was. The colour of the offspring of yellow parents reared on yellow sand (top panel, top right) was almost pure yellow.

These experiments – and others that Kammerer conducted – seemed to prove conclusively that acquired characteristics could be inherited. Such a proof would revolutionise genetics, and Kammerer's results deserved – at the very least – careful scrutiny. Instead his work was greeted by the scientific community with a malicious derision that drove him, in the end, to suicide.

Above and below: two of the many distinct and specialised finch species that occur on the Galapagos Islands. Darwin cited these birds as evidence for evolution

Genesis. But this is completely unnecessary, even for those who accept the authority of the Bible. In fact, there is surprisingly little conflict between modern scientific theories of the development of the Universe and the sequence of events described in the first chapter of Genesis.

The Universe is generally supposed by physicists to have originated with an enormous primordial explosion. As the Universe began to cool down after this 'big bang', matter in the form of atoms condensed from the incandescent plasma, and vast gas clouds gave rise to galaxies of stars. Relatively small bodies of hot matter were then captured by the gravitational pull of the stars and became planets orbiting around them. One such was the Earth. As the Earth cooled, the water vapour condensed and gave rise to the seas. Life originated in the water, and among the earliest living organisms were plants capable of photosynthesis. Animals arose first in the sea, and later colonised the dry land. From these land animals in the fullness of time, Man evolved.

The first chapter of Genesis describes a similar sequence: first the separation of light from darkness – or in other words, of radiation from matter. Then the separation of the Earth as a single mass from the heavens, and the subsequent appearance of the seas and dry land. Then the origin of plants, then of animals in the sea, then of land animals, and finally of Man.

These two descriptions of the origins of things differ in that the scientific one supposes that the time scale was of thousands of millions of years, whereas the Bible speaks of the different stages as taking place on different days. If the term 'day' is interpreted to mean an age, there need be little conflict between the two accounts. The main discrepancy is that in Genesis, the Sun and Moon appear only on the fourth 'day'. But this in itself is significant in that it shows that the term 'day' is not to be taken literally, for it could not possibly have a literal meaning if the Sun, by the rising or setting of which days are measured, did not yet exist, according to the very same text. Moreover, other passages in the Bible make it perfectly plain that human measurements of time are not the same as divine ones. 'One day is with the Lord as a thousand years, and a thousand years as one day.'

In the end, it seems that the protracted controversy between biblical fundamentalists and evolutionists, so often portrayed as a dramatic confrontation of science and religion, comes down to little more than a dispute over the meaning of the word 'day' in a context that provides no basis for assuming that a day must consist of 24 hours. Thus there seem to be no good grounds, even religious ones, for rejecting the theory of evolution by descent.

However, a new series of controversies springs up as soon as we accept this theory. Once again, underlying many of them are religious and philosophical questions, although on the surface they may seem to be purely scientific.

The most important of these controversies concerns the origin of new species: do

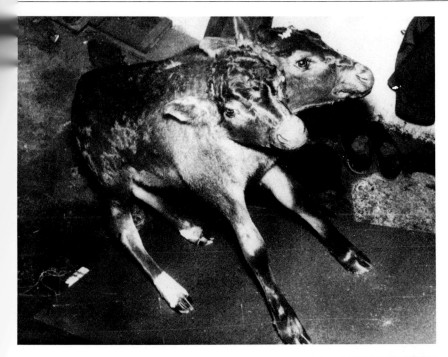

they come into being gradually, or as a result of sudden 'sports' or jumps? This question has been hotly debated for over a hundred years. The two schools of thought are usually referred to as gradualism and punctuationalism.

Darwin himself was a gradualist, and so are his modern followers, the neo-Darwinians. Their reasons for adopting this point of view are more philosophical than scientific.

Even before the publication of *Origin of species*, several writers pointed out that the theory of evolution did not contradict the idea of the creation of species by God, because God might just as well make a new species by transforming an existing one as by forming it directly from non-living matter. On this view, the Creator was continually guiding the evolutionary process and making new species through it. One advantage of this interpretation was that it supplied a ready explanation for the relatively sudden appearance of new kinds of animals and plants.

On the other hand, those who espoused the philosophy of materialism had to try to explain the process of evolution in terms of the laws of matter alone, and were at pains to reject anything that smacked of the miraculous. Darwin himself favoured gradualism because of his materialist presuppositions, and rejected the idea of sudden changes because, as he wrote in *Origin of species*, it 'seems to me to enter into the realms of miracle, and to leave those of science'.

Although such philosophical views have continued to play a hidden but important role in the debate, there is no real reason for the belief in a Creator to lead to a denial of the gradual evolution of new species, or on the other hand for a materialist to deny sudden jumps in evolution. Surprisingly the two concepts can be reconciled. There are in fact

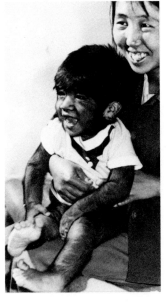

Top: this two-headed calf was the result of a genetic mutation. It lived for only a few days

Above: a hairy boy born in north-eastern China in 1977. Strange features such as this can arise through chance combinations of genes, but are unlikely to be favoured by natural selection

Right: an ancon, or short-legged sheep, compared with a normal sheep. Genetic engineering was practised long before the theory was known: the ancon species was bred from a single ram-lamb born in 1791

theologians who argue that God created the different forms of life by setting up the Universe and the laws of nature, including the possibility of random genetic change, in the first place in such a way that evolution was bound to occur exactly as neo-Darwinians think it does. By contrast, some materialists accept the idea of sudden large changes, but regard them as random.

Now, leaving aside these philosophical questions, we can turn to the factual evidence concerning the origin of new species.

The main argument used by Darwin in favour of gradualism relied on an analogy with the development of breeds of domesticated animals, such as dogs, pigeons and rabbits, and varieties of cultivated plants, such as cabbages, dahlias and grapes, by the agency of human selection. He reasoned that just as animal and plant breeders select favourable specimens as parents of the next generation, and thus gradually improve the breed or variety in a particular direction, so in the wild natural selection would result in parents well-adapted to the conditions of life leaving more offspring than those less well-adapted. There would thus be a progressive improvement in the adaptation of the race to its environment.

However, the controversial question is not how locally adapted races arise *within* species, but how species themselves originate. Ironically, this is the very question that Darwin failed to answer satisfactorily in *Origin of species*. He simply assumed, as his followers also assume, that the same kinds of process continued over long periods of time would lead to the gradual divergence of races into new species. No one disputes that this may sometimes occur, but the opponents of gradualism claim that many, if not most, species arise much more quickly, by relatively large and sudden transformations.

This case, like Darwin's own, can be based on an analogy with the breeding of domesticated animals and plants. For while

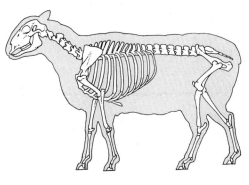

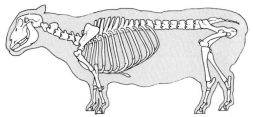

some new varieties or strains have been produced gradually by long-continued selection, others have originated suddenly from occasional 'sports' or freaks. In fruit trees, for example, peculiar shoots sometimes appear, differing from all the others, from which new varieties can be propagated. In the history of animal breeding too, new breeds have been started from spontaneously occurring freaks.

If in the course of evolution, freaks or sports produced by wild animals and plants occasionally survived and managed to breed successfully, a distinct new type derived from the original species could come into existence more or less suddenly. For example, it seems probable that a fossil rhino genus called *Teleoceras* originated in this way. These dwarf, short-legged rhinos resemble ancon sheep and, like them, may have appeared suddenly as a result of a genetic mutation leading to the improper development of cartilage at the end of bones, a condition known as achondroplasia. If this were so, we would not expect to find in the fossil record a whole range of intermediate types between *Teleoceras* and the rhino species from which it evolved.

No missing links have been found. As a general rule, in the fossil record new species appear, continue relatively unchanged for maybe several million years, and then become extinct. There is little evidence to support the gradualist view. Darwin argued that this was due to the imperfection of the fossil record, but after 120 years of further research, this argument is wearing rather thin.

Furthermore, calculations of the rates of evolutionary change, based on data from fossil horses and other groups of animals, have shown that they are much too slow to be able to account for the gradual appearance of all the different kinds of organisms in the time available, long though it has been. The neo-Darwinians reply that gradual changes

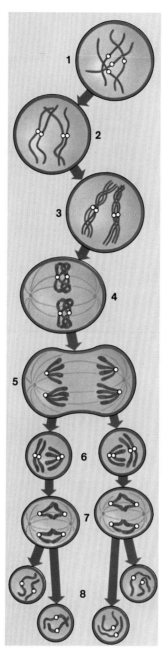

might have been much less slow at some periods than others. But in admitting this, they shift their position so that it comes much closer to the idea of discontinuous or sudden changes.

One of the most convincing reasons for thinking that sudden jumps occur is that many present-day species differ from more or less closely related species in the number and structure of their chromosomes. Changes in chromosomes of these types are known to occur occasionally during the process of cell division, known as meiosis, that produces egg and sperm cells. The chromosomes of the mother cell come together in pairs at the beginning of meiosis, and normally one of each pair then moves into each of the two daughter cells. But sometimes pairs fail to separate properly, and one daughter cell gets too many chromosomes, and the other too few. Consequently offspring derived from these abnormal cells have the wrong number of chromosomes. They are often both abnormal and sterile as a consequence; but if they do manage to breed, either through self-fertilisation, as commonly occurs in plants, or by crossing with similarly abnormal organisms (their own brothers or sisters, for instance), they may give rise to a new species straight away; the differences in chromosome numbers set up barriers to interbreeding and keep the new type separate from the parent species. Other chromosomal changes during meiosis involving the breaking and rejoining of chromosomes in the wrong places can have a similar effect.

Hopeful monsters

Those who advocate sudden jumps in evolution do not deny that the great majority of freakish organisms will be weeded out by natural selection. On the long time scale of evolution, it is sufficient that only very rarely are 'hopeful monsters' able to survive and reproduce. Even neo-Darwinians can hardly deny that this might have happened. The two schools of thought differ mainly in their emphasis, one considering that sudden jumps have played little part in the evolution of new species and the other claiming that many, if not most, new types have arisen in this way. On balance, the available evidence supports the second of these views, although a great deal of work remains to be done.

This is what the current controversy among evolutionary theorists is all about. At first sight it is puzzling that these issues should raise such passionate feelings. But as in earlier controversies, some of the contenders are fighting to defend not just scientific theories but their fundamental beliefs. This time, however, it is the materialists who feel threatened by the challenge to orthodoxy.

Above: a diagram of the process of *meiosis*, which occurs in the production of sex cells. Chromosomes pair (1 and 2), become double-stranded (3) and thicken, exchanging segments of their strands to mix the genetic information (4); the pairs separate (5), and the cell divides (6). The two-stranded chromosomes in each cell divide and the cells split (7). The resultant cells (8) have half the number of chromosomes of the parent cell. This number redoubles in sexual reproduction

Left: smooth hawksbeard, a result of faulty meiosis

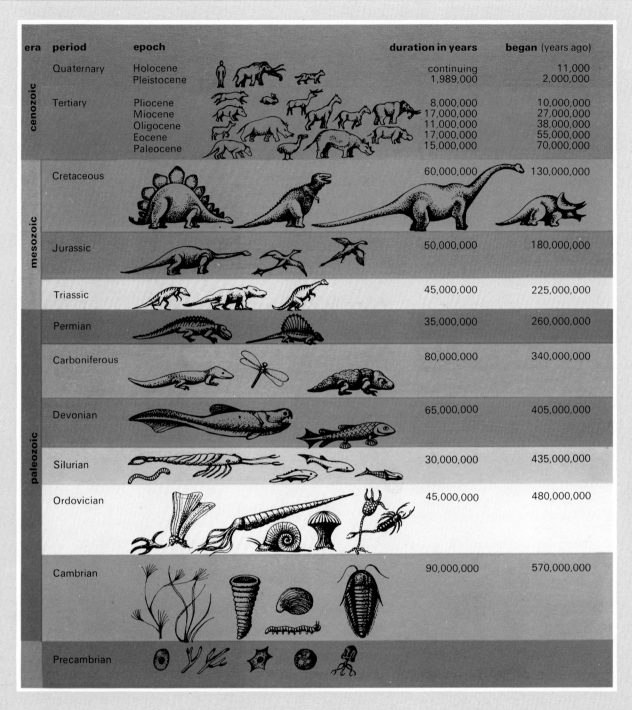

era	period	epoch		duration in years	began (years ago)
cenozoic	Quaternary	Holocene		continuing	11,000
		Pleistocene		1,989,000	2,000,000
	Tertiary	Pliocene		8,000,000	10,000,000
		Miocene		17,000,000	27,000,000
		Oligocene		11,000,000	38,000,000
		Eocene		17,000,000	55,000,000
		Paleocene		15,000,000	70,000,000
mesozoic	Cretaceous			60,000,000	130,000,000
	Jurassic			50,000,000	180,000,000
	Triassic			45,000,000	225,000,000
paleozoic	Permian			35,000,000	260,000,000
	Carboniferous			80,000,000	340,000,000
	Devonian			65,000,000	405,000,000
	Silurian			30,000,000	435,000,000
	Ordovician			45,000,000	480,000,000
	Cambrian			90,000,000	570,000,000
	Precambrian				

The evolution of animal life on Earth as shown by fossils. Most of the animals shown here are extinct, but scientists know about them because they were preserved as fossils. Life is thought to have begun in water, so early fossils are all of animals which lived there. Little evidence remains of life from Precambrian times when they were soft and mostly one-celled, but by the Cambrian period more advanced water animals had evolved. Fish, the first backboned animals, appeared in the early Silurian period, but animals first ventured onto land in the Devonian age when insects appeared. By the Carboniferous period, there were land animals with backbones – amphibians. Later the first reptiles appeared and for the next 120 million years they were the ruling animals of land and sea – the age of the dinosaurs. Flying reptiles appeared in the Jurassic period, one group of these giving rise to birds. At the end of the Mesozoic era the climate changed and most of the reptiles disappeared, replaced by the mammals which began to evolve from the Cretaceous age onwards into the many forms of today. Man began to evolve about 14 million years ago.

Nothing but machines?

The theory of neo-Darwinism is regarded by many scientists almost as an article of faith, but it is by no means certain that it can explain the sheer diversity of living things on Earth

LIKE DARWIN'S ORIGINAL THEORY of evolution, the neo-Darwinian theory currently accepted by scientists attributes an essential role to natural selection. This principle in itself is obvious enough: it simply states that organisms vary and that the variations tend to be inherited by their offspring; that organisms generally produce more offspring than can possibly survive; and that the offspring best adapted to their environment will usually be the ones that survive to reproduce. Thus natural selection ensures that favourable variations will tend to accumulate in the population.

Darwin himself believed that, whereas some hereditary variations are due to chance, others are due to adaptations acquired by ancestors in response to their environments. For example, plants grown in hot, dry places generally develop thicker leaves than plants of the same species grown in cooler and moister conditions, and intelligent animals placed in new environments develop new habits appropriate to their circumstances. Darwin considered that such acquired characteristics could be inherited, and he even thought up an elaborate theory, which he called the theory of pangenesis, to explain how this might happen. He suggested that small particles from all over the body moved into the egg and sperm cells, modifying them in accordance with the structures and habits the organisms had acquired. This theory was subsequently proved wrong.

Nevertheless, if acquired characteristics are not inherited, it is difficult to understand why many features of living organisms have developed. Camels, for example, have pads of thickened skin on their knees. It is easy to see how they are acquired in response to the abrasion of the skin as the animals kneel down. But baby camels are born with them.

The neo-Darwinian theory differs from Darwin's in that it takes into account the theories of genetics, a science Darwin knew nothing of. (Gregor Mendel conducted his pioneering experiments in genetics in 1865, but his results remained unknown until 1900. Charles Darwin died in 1882.) According to genetics, inheritance can be explained in terms of genes, made up of the chemical DNA and strung together in long thread-like chromosomes within the nuclei of cells (see page 16). The genes in the sex cells are not changed by alterations in other parts of the body that occur in response to the conditions of life. Because the inheritance of acquired characteristics cannot be understood in terms of genetics, its very *possibility* is denied by neo-Darwinians, on theoretical grounds.

The hereditary differences between organisms are explained by neo-Darwinians in terms of random, accidental changes in the genes, called genetic mutations. Thus, according to this theory, camels are born with pads on their knees not because of the inheritance of this characteristic as a result of the habit of kneeling, but because of random mutations that just happened to give rise to pads in the right places. The only other source of hereditary variation admitted by this orthodox view is the random shuffling of genes produced by the two parents in the process of sexual reproduction.

In summary, neo-Darwinism states that evolutionary creativity depends on nothing but blind chance, combined with the necessities imposed on organisms by natural selection. There is no plan or direction to the

process of evolution, and living beings, including human beings, have no ultimate purpose except to survive and reproduce.

The evangelists of neo-Darwinism usually present their theory as if it were an established scientific fact that any rational person is bound to accept, whether he or she likes it or not. However, this is far from being the case, for four main reasons.

First, although natural selection will undoubtedly filter out organisms that are poorly adapted to their environment, and so will tend to lead to the development of locally adapted races *within* species, there is no evidence that fundamentally new types of organism develop gradually through the selection of small variations. For example, we cannot ascertain from the fossil record how complex structures such as the eyes of vertebrate animals or the feathers of birds originated. They could just as well have appeared by sudden jumps as by a long-continued process of gradual modification. Darwin and his followers prefer the idea of gradual changes because they wish to avoid anything that might seem miraculous, as we have seen. But this is nothing more than intellectual prejudice, and armchair speculations about hypothetical missing links do not prove anything one way or another.

Secondly, if the origin of species has occurred gradually under the influence of natural selection, the characteristics of the species should be specifically adapted to the conditions of life. But many features of animals and plants seem to exist for no

Left: an artist's impression of the landscape of the Earth as it cooled after the 'big bang'. Life probably evolved in a 'primordial broth' containing amino acids formed from the atmospheric gases by flashes of lightning. But does this really mean that all living creatures are nothing more than complex chemical structures?

Far left: a fox scavenges from an overturned dustbin in a town habitat. Can it really be, as neo-Darwinists claim, that the programme for such intelligent adaptation is encoded in the genes?

Below left: Arabian camels. Adult camels have hard pads on their knees. It is easy enough to suppose that they might have arisen through abrasion as the camels knelt down – but baby camels are born with them. If, as neo-Darwinists believe, acquired characteristics cannot be inherited, how can this be?

Below: in an astonishing camouflage manoeuvre, the butterflies on the right mimic those on the left. In many cases, the mimicked species is distasteful to the mimics' predators

particular reason. In the plant kingdom, for example, species with many different kinds of leaves and flowers seem to survive equally well in the same environment; so how could similar selection pressures have given rise to such widely different forms? In a detailed study of a family of tropical water snails, the *Podostemaceae*, the eminent botanist J. C. Willis concluded that, although an enormous variety of forms was shown by the different species, 'there was no evidence to be found that would show that natural selection had anything to do with the multiplicity of form in these plants, for all were growing under the same conditions.' This led him to remark that 'it would almost seem as if, in cases like this, if not perhaps in most, evolution must go on, whether there be any adaptational reason for it or not.'

Thirdly, the genetic theory provides an inadequate explanation of heredity. It takes no account of the results of experiments that show that organisms may develop under influences from previous members of their species, influences that are transmitted directly through morphogenic fields (or form fields). If they do in fact draw on a sort of pooled 'species memory', then acquired characteristics could indeed be inherited without the need for modification of the genetic chemical, DNA. Thus, for example, animals could 'tune in' to the experience of previous animals and benefit from it.

Lastly, neo-Darwinism depends on a very questionable theory of the nature of life, the mechanistic theory. This is based on the assumption that living organisms are nothing but complex machines, governed only by the known laws of chemistry and physics.

It is because of this assumption that most biologists reject the existence of telepathy,

precognition, psychokinesis, and indeed the whole range of the so-called paranormal. This refusal is not based on an examination of the facts, but merely on the grounds that because these things cannot at present be explained, they cannot possibly happen.

There is, of course, no reason to suppose that we already know all the fundamental laws of matter and energy; quite apart from the existence of so many unexplained phenomena, the continued existence of scientific research itself indicates that we do not. If the hypothesis of morphogenetic fields could be confirmed by experiment, it would involve the discovery of a new set of laws providing connections between things across space and time – laws that have not yet been recognised by science. And still more laws may be discovered in the future, whose existence has not so far even been suspected.

The mechanistic theory of life is founded on an analogy between living organisms and machines; for example, the eye is compared

Above: a shore crab that has lost a pincer grows a new one. Orthodox science has not yet come up with an explanation of how this regeneration is possible

Left: a peacock with its magnificent tail fanned out as part of the courtship ritual. How would 'survival of the fittest' result in such unnecessarily complex forms?

Below: the elegant 'zip-fastener' structure of a bird's feather, which is designed to provide the bird with a waterproof coat. Did it evolve gradually, as the neo-Darwinists believe, or could it have appeared by a sudden jump at some point in their history?

to a camera, and the brain to a computer. Such similarities do indeed exist, but they do not prove that living organisms are *nothing but* machines.

Both living organisms and machines are purposeful. But the purposes of machines are given them by the human beings who design them; for example, the functions computers perform depend on the way they are designed and programmed. But what designs and programmes living organisms? Mechanists reply that nothing does: it all happens as a result of chance mutations and natural selection. But this is a circular argument: the neo-Darwinian theory of evolution depends on assuming that the machine theory of life is correct, and this theory can be justified only in terms of the neo-Darwinian theory of evolution.

The most important argument mechanists use to justify their position is to state that, since living organisms are made up of identifiable chemicals and obey the known laws of physics, they cannot involve any principles that science has not already discovered. The easiest way to see the flaw in this reasoning is to consider the mechanistic theory of the origin of life.

It is generally thought that the first living cells appeared over two and a half thousand million years ago in a 'primordial broth' containing organic chemicals, such as amino acids, formed from gases in the atmosphere by huge flashes of lightning. This theory is fairly plausible, but of course we can never know for sure what happened in the remote past. There will always be a possibility that life originated somewhere else in the Universe, and that the Earth was 'seeded' with primitive organisms that came – or were deliberately sent – from outside.

However, let us assume for the purposes of argument that the first cells arose from originally non-living aggregates of chemicals. Now mechanists assert that this shows that there is nothing in life that is not already present in non-living matter. They often claim, in addition, that it should eventually

Below: honey bees at work in a hive. Individual bees instinctively act for the good of the hive even if, by doing so, they endanger their own lives. Can this behaviour be explained in terms of the mechanistic view of life favoured by the neo-Darwinists?

Bottom: a tiger resting in long grass. Camouflage colouring can be extremely effective, and it is plausible to argue that it must have arisen through the process of natural selection in response to environmental pressures. But can this kind of argument be extended to include *all* characteristics of living things?

the chemistry of its components alone. Likewise, the fact that living organisms are made up of chemicals, and may have originated from non-living components in the first place, does not prove that they can be understood merely in terms of chemistry.

Now imagine someone who refused to believe this. He might try to prove his point by building a replica of a set from parts he had made himself using simple raw materials. When he succeeded in doing this, and found that it worked just like the original, he might regard this as a conclusive demonstration that it involved nothing but the parts he had put together. Nevertheless, in spite of his technical achievement, he would still not know anything about radio waves. Similarly, even if living organisms were ever to be synthesised artificially, this would not prove that they were nothing but chemical systems.

Continuing mysteries

Apart from the logical flaws, the most serious defect of the mechanistic theory is that it has failed to lead to an understanding of the central problems of biology. After decades of intensive research, it is still not known how animals and plants manage to take up the forms characteristic of their species – think of an orchid, a peacock, or a tiger – starting from egg cells. Nor is it understood how they are able to regenerate after damage: a flat-worm, for example, can be cut up into several pieces, each of which will grow into a complete worm. And the instincts of animals – the behaviour of ants in a colony for example – has continued to be inexplicable in mechanistic terms, despite extensive research.

Mechanists concede that these phenomena cannot be explained in terms of physics and chemistry at present, but they say that this is only because they are so complicated. They assert that it will be possible to explain them mechanistically at some time in the future. But this is not a scientific argument based on evidence; it is nothing more than a statement of faith in the mechanistic creed.

Thus, while the neo-Darwinian theory seems to be based on well-established facts, with all the authority of objective science behind it, on closer examination it turns out to be nothing of the sort. Indeed, behind its scientific façade, it appears to have become for many of its followers remarkably like a religion. This seems to be the reason why they propagate their dogmas so zealously, guard against heresies so vigilantly, and deny the truth of all other faiths so vehemently. Nevertheless, it is perfectly possible to accept the idea of evolution without having to believe the neo-Darwinian doctrine. Evolution may not be blind and purposeless – and the amazing creativity of the living world may have more behind it than mere chance.

be possible to make living organisms artificially from chemicals in a test-tube, and that this would prove that they are nothing but complicated chemical systems.

To see the fallacy in this, consider the analogy of a transistor radio. The set is made up of wires, transistors and so on, and contains a battery with chemicals inside it. Before all these different components were assembled, they did not function as a radio, picking up radio signals and turning them into sounds. But after they have been put together in the right way, they do so. The chemical composition of the parts does not change when they are wired up together in the set, nor does the set gain weight when it is picking up transmissions. But this does not mean that the set can be explained in terms of

Is life nothing more than matter in motion? Is mental activity merely a process of electrical reactions within the brain? Or could there be some altogether more mysterious force at work?

HOW DID THE CORALS come to have their many and varied forms? How did the first magnolia flowers appear? How did spiders start to spin webs? How did the first birds begin to fly?

Countless similar questions could be asked. For example, there are over a million living species of insects, and all of them have their own intricate inborn patterns of behaviour enabling them to feed, survive, find mates and reproduce. The evolutionary process has been one of prodigious creativity that, throughout the long history of life, has thrown up hundreds of millions of new kinds of animals and plants.

Our minds are hardly capable of comprehending this. We can understand to some extent how things are repeated, but not how they come into being for the first time. Generally speaking, nature is repetitive. Animals and plants generally reproduce organisms of their own kinds: carrot plants come from carrot seeds, baby hamsters from hamsters, and canaries from canary eggs. They inherit their genes from their parents, and may also 'tune in' to morphogenetic fields that shape them as they develop through the embryonic stages into adults, as we have seen. In their instinctive behaviour, animals repeat the actions and movements performed by countless generations of their predecessors. They run, as it were, in grooves of inherited habit.

Some of the shapes and instincts that turn up in certain species in the course of evolution may even be derived from those of other species living in other parts of the world. In Australia, for instance, there were until recent times no placental mammals. Instead, the marsupials – pouched animals, the group to which kangaroos belong – evolved to produce a range of species that duplicated in remarkable ways the characteristics of mammals elsewhere in the world. There were pouched versions of wolves, cats, ant-eaters, moles, flying squirrels, and so on. Conceivably, these marsupials somehow 'tuned in' to the morphogenetic fields of comparable mammals living on other continents. Likewise, some cases of evolutionary atavism, in which species reproduce features of other species long since extinct, may be due to their picking up a sort of 'ancestral memory' by the process of morphic resonance. Horses, for instance, are sometimes born with two toes, like their distant ancestors.

But even these speculations would still

Above: a pair of blind cave characins. These fish live in dark caves in Mexico where they do not need to see – and their eyes, because they are redundant, have disappeared. It is easy to see how such changes evolve in response to environmental pressures – but harder to understand how the complex forms of living creatures evolved in the first place. It is possible that some traits may develop through a method of 'tuning in' to members of other species

provide explanations in terms of the repetition of precedents. They would not explain how new patterns or structures or instincts arose for the first time. It is indeed in the very nature of scientific theories that they deal with the repetitive aspects of nature. Scientific laws are concerned with regularities. They cannot explain happenings that are unique and unprecedented; they cannot account for creativity, which is in its very essence unpredictable.

The same is true of human creativity.

A European field mouse (left); and an Australian marsupial mouse (below), which carries its young in its pouch. Could morphic resonance account for the similarity of these species?

Right: Jacques Monod, a biochemist and supporter of a mechanistic philosophy

Countless people use bicycles, aeroplanes, televisions, cars and computers. It is fairly easy to learn how to operate them, and even how to make them; these are matters of following established procedures, repeating what has been done before. But at one time none of these machines had even been dreamed of. They were all invented, and their inventors were men who thought of new possibilities, and did things that no one had ever done before.

Likewise, Newton thought of the theory of gravitation for the first time: it was original; no one had known it before him. But now it is learned by school children all over the world. Mozart composed music that no one had ever heard before, but that is now played by thousands of musicians.

Once something new has come into the world, it can be repeated, and science helps us understand the processes of repetition. But creativity cannot be understood in terms of repetition, and poses a problem that lies outside the scope of science. It can be thought about only in terms of more far-reaching theories of reality, namely philosophical theories.

All of us have some sort of philosophy through which we interpret the world, whether we are aware of it or not. Human creativity can be explained by four totally different philosophical systems. The first is philosophical materialism.

Matter and its movements

Philosophical materialism derives from the assumption that only matter is real, and that everything can ultimately be explained in terms of matter and its movements. This is the philosophy that underlies the mechanistic theory of life and the neo-Darwinian theory of evolution (see page 20). A particularly clear statement of this position has been put forward by the late Jacques Monod, a molecular biologist, in his book *Chance and necessity*.

In the 19th century, the materialist doctrine seemed quite straightforward. Matter was thought to be made up of solid atoms, like tiny billiard balls, whose movement was inexorably determined by physical laws. But this simple view has been superseded by the advances of modern physics. Atoms are now known to split up into other particles, and these can fragment into still smaller ones, and so on. Moreover, such particles are no longer thought of as solid, but as ceaselessly vibrating forms of energy. Physical changes are no longer regarded as fully determined by identifiable causes; there is an element of unpredictability in everything. So materialism has become much vaguer than it used to be, because it is no longer possible to say exactly what matter is or how it behaves.

Nevertheless, many materialists still cling to a basic belief that there is no such thing as God, or spirit, or indeed anything other than matter in motion. Consequently, they deny that the human mind involves anything more than the physical functioning of the brain; they claim that the mind can have no influence on human behaviour, because it cannot be analysed in terms of physics and chemistry. Consciousness is regarded as a kind of shadow that runs parallel to changes in the brain, or as an inexplicable aspect of the chemical and electrical activity of the nerves.

Because materialists deny that there is any non-physical creative principle either in the Universe as a whole, or in the human brain, the only reason they can give for the creativity of the evolutionary process, or for human creativity, is *chance*. They believe that the evolution of the Universe and of life within it is entirely blind and purposeless, the result of a series of meaningless accidents. And of course they can give no explanation for the origin of the Universe to start with, nor for the particular physical

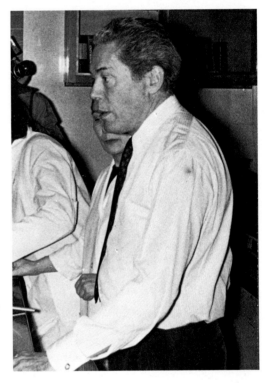

laws that govern its continued existence.

This doctrine can only mean that materialists' own lives are due to nothing but the interplay of chance and physical necessity, and their own thoughts and beliefs (including the belief in materialism itself) are the inevitable result of physical processes in their brains, over which they have no conscious control.

Needless to say, none of this can be proved either by science or by logic. It can only be accepted as an act of faith.

The idea that the mind is not material in nature but nevertheless interacts with the body is more in accordance with common sense than the materialist doctrine. This position is known as dualism, or interactionism. One of its best-known exponents is

Left: these Japanese monkeys have learned to avoid the cold of winter by immersing themselves in hot spring-water. It is impossible to predict what will happen next in the creative process of evolution: will this change in habit give rise to new physical traits – and perhaps a new species?

Above right: the philosopher Henri Bergson (1859–1941), who believed that the astonishing diversity of living creatures on the Earth could be explained only by the existence of a creative force, the *élan vital*, that drives the process of evolution onwards

Right: an addict injects himself with heroin – producing extraordinary changes in his mental state

the philosopher Sir Karl Popper.

The interaction of the mind and the body can be thought of by analogy with a driver in a car. The driver's actions on the controls – the way he steers, changes gear, accelerates and brakes – affect the way the car moves. Conversely, things going on outside the car on the road, and changes inside it revealed by dials on the dashboard, influence the driver's decisions and actions.

Likewise, the mind controls the body, and what is going on in the outside world and within the body itself influence the mind. But not everything going on in the mind need be paralleled by changes in the brain, just as not everything the driver thinks about need be paralleled by changes in the car. For example, he might stop the car and leave its engine ticking over while he looks at a map. Obviously, under these conditions, there is no direct relationship between the vibrations of the engine and his thoughts as he plans his route.

Thus, the mind can function independently of the brain, although it must act through it, just as the driver can function independently of his car, although he can only drive about by using it.

If the independence of the mind is admitted, the creativity of human beings can be explained in terms of the powers of the mind, rather than in terms of chance events within the brain, as materialists suppose. And if the creative activity of the mind is accepted, then it is possible to consider that the invention of new patterns of behaviour not only in Man,

Below: Sir Karl Popper, a leading exponent of the theory of life that holds that the body and the mind interact one with the other

but also in the higher animals, depends on mental processes. It is possible that this is true to some extent even of the lower animals.

But there is a limit to how far this explanation of creativity can be pushed. It does not make much sense to say that the development of new *forms* of animals depends on the creative mental activity of embryos, and still less can this be said of the evolution of new kinds of plants.

Thus, although supporters of this philosophical position are able to attribute human inventiveness to the creative power of the mind, and to some extent account for the appearance of new types of behaviour in animals in a similar way, they cannot explain the creativity of the evolutionary process as a whole in these terms. Here, for lack of anything better, they fall back on to the materialist doctrine of chance.

The third kind of philosophy rejects materialism entirely. It proposes that life as a whole has a creativity within it that cannot be explained in terms of physical laws. It is this creative principle that causes animals and plants to take up new forms, and that gives rise to the amazing diversity of species. It also lies at the root of new instincts; it works more freely in the higher animals as the source of their intelligence, and acts through the human mind to inspire new thoughts.

The best known version of this philosophy is that of Henri Bergson, who in his book *Creative evolution* proposed the existence of a vital impetus, the *élan vital*, driving forward the evolutionary process.

There is no need to assume that the activity of such a creative principle is expressed continuously. Most of the time, organisms simply take on the forms of their forbears, and repeat the same patterns of behaviour. But sometimes they are prevented from doing this, either because they find themselves in an abnormal environment, or because they have a genetic defect that disturbs their normal development. Think, for example, of animals born with defective eyesight as a result of random genetic mutations. In most cases they will simply perish. But occasionally one may develop a new way of behaving, relying much more on the sense of hearing than normal animals of its species. Consequently, it may be able to function much better in the dark,

and this may actually be of advantage at night, or in environments such as dark caves. If so, this new pattern of behaviour will be favoured by natural selection.

It is important to recognise that, although this new pattern of behaviour arose in response to a random mutation in the DNA, it cannot be explained in terms of the mutation alone. To see this point more clearly, think of the way in which people respond to injuries. For example, a man maimed in an accident and incapable of doing a normal job may take up painting and produce impressive works of art. In one sense, the accidental injury was a cause of his painting, because he would never have done it otherwise, but his creative response to his new circumstances was not a direct physical consequence of the injury. Likewise, the creative responses of animals and plants to random mutations are not a simple physical result of the change in their DNA. Mutations and changed environments provide challenges to which organisms may or may not respond creatively. Here, as elsewhere, necessity is the mother of invention. And then not all inventions are successful; most are not, and are weeded out by natural selection.

An ultimate purpose?

The notion that evolutionary creativity depends on a creative principle inherent in nature does not in itself mean that evolution has any particular goal. Nor does it account for the origin of the Universe in which this creativity is expressed. This philosophy in fact represents a kind of pantheism, in which nature is seen as the body of a God continuously developing and creating himself, but always heading into the unknown, without any ultimate purpose or goal.

The fourth philosophical position embraces all the previous ones: it accepts the reality of matter, as materialism does; it accepts the reality of the mind, as interactionism does; and it also accepts the existence of an inherent creativity in nature, as pantheism does. But it goes further in that it suggests the existence of a creative consciousness that transcends the Universe, and that is the source of its existence and of the laws that govern it. This divine consciousness also constitutes the goal towards which the evolutionary process is drawn in an ever more conscious manner. In Teilhard de Chardin's Christian evolutionary philosophy, put forward in *The phenomenon of Man*, this supremely conscious goal is called the 'omega point'.

This interpretation of evolution in terms of the creative activity of a God both within and beyond the Universe is just as compatible with the scientifically established facts as the three other philosophies considered above. Science itself provides no grounds for choosing one of them rather than another. This is a personal choice, and entirely a matter of faith.

Fallacies and absurdities

One of the more entertaining aspects of neo-Darwinism is its tendency to get entangled in self-contradiction. Darwin himself wondered if the mind of Man could be trusted since it had, as he believed, descended 'from the lowest animal'. According to Darwinist theory, the mind *must* have evolved as a means to survival – not as a creative agent with the potential for arriving at the truth of any sort. And if that is the case, mechanistic biologists have no reason to believe in *any* scientific theory, including their own, for the mind of Man is no more than a 'useless' evolutionary accident.

Perhaps most astonishing is the suggestion that consciousness (i.e. the mind) actually does not exist, since it is not detectable by physics or chemistry. 'Actually there is no such thing,' states neurologist L.S. Kubie. When philosopher Michael Polanyi objected to the absurdity of regarding humans as insentient automata, neurologist R.W. Gerard retorted: 'One thing we know, ideas don't move muscles!' If that were true, Gerard would have been unable to utter a word.

**'Unimaginative almost to coldness'
was how French educationalist
Hippolyte Rivail was once
described – yet, as Allan Kardec,
he was to lead millions to
Spiritism.** GUY LYON PLAYFAIR
outlines Kardec's life and work

HIPPOLYTE LEON DENIZARD RIVAIL, better
known today under the pseudonym of 'Allan
Kardec', was born in Lyon, France, in 1804.
His father, a distinguished local lawyer and
judge, wanted him to have the best education
available, so at the age of 10 he was sent to the
Yverdon Institute in Switzerland, founded
and run by J.H. Pestalozzi (1746–1827), the
man often credited with having revo-
lutionised European education.

Believing intuition to be the source of all
knowledge, Pestalozzi encouraged his pupils
to develop as individuals, while submitting
them to a formidable daily regime that included 10 hours of lessons over the full range of
the arts and sciences. Religious instruction
was also available for those who, like Rivail,
came from Roman Catholic families.

Rivail's six-year stay at Yverdon profoundly influenced the course of his life. He
soon decided to become a teacher, in order to
carry on Pestalozzi's work in France, open-
ing his own school in Paris in 1826. By then,
he had already published the first of an
eventual total of 22 textbooks on French
grammar, mathematics and educational
reform. He also began a series of free public
educational courses in the sciences, which he
kept going for 10 years.

A modest beginning
Forced to close his school in 1834 for financial reasons, Rivail had to work as an accoun-
tant to keep himself and his wife alive,
though he still gave free private lessons in his
own home, and by the early 1850s, when his
career underwent a dramatic change, he was
well-established as a progressive, free-
thinking writer and educator. Anna Black-
well, who translated some of his later books
into English, remembered him as 'more like a
German than a Frenchman'. He was, she
wrote, a man of energy and perseverance, but
'unimaginative almost to coldness, incredu-
lous by nature and by education', and 'a
close, logical reasoner'. He lived a quiet,
modest and hard-working life, and does not
sound at all like a man who would become
involved in the founding of a new religious
philosophy.

But events had taken place in 1848 in the
United States that were to change Rivail's
entire philosophy and influence that of millions of others. It was in the home of the Fox
family in Hydesville, New York, that tables
moved seemingly of their own accord and
mysterious rappings were heard, apparently
emanating from 'spirits' of the dead. This
marked the beginning of the Spiritualist

Above: the founder of the
Spiritist movement, Allan
Kardec

Below: title page of Kardec's
massive seminal work *The
spirits' book*, published in
France in 1857

movement, which was to become all the rage
in Paris, as in other European cities.

Before long, as a contemporary journalist
put it, there was scarcely a table between
Montmartre and the Champs-Elysées remaining unturned.

Rivail, despite his wide-ranging interests,
was at first extremely sceptical. 'If you have
studied the sciences, you will laugh at the
superstitious credulity of the ignorant, and
will no longer believe in ghosts,' he had
written in one of his early textbooks, and
when in 1854 a friend told him that tables
were not only jumping off the floor, but
beating out messages from the dead, Rivail
replied tersely: 'I will believe that only when
I see it.'

He seems to have been in no hurry to see
it, for it was not until the following year that
he finally went along to a seance, where he
saw a demonstration of 'basket writing', an
early form of automatic writing in which
sitters' hands were placed on a basket
through which a pencil was driven. 'I could
see,' he recalled later, 'that there was something serious behind all this apparent

triviality . . . like the revelation of a new law, which I decided to investigate thoroughly.'

This he promptly did, and he soon noticed that whereas messages received at the sittings he attended were often frivolous, they would invariably take on a serious tone when addressed to him personally. Then his friend, the playwright Victorien Sardou, asked him to look through some notebooks kept by a group with which he had been studying spirit phenomena for five years. Rivail was at once impressed by 'the knowledge and the charity that shine out from the serious communications', and he embarked on a very intense series of sittings with a medium named Japhet, in which he put a number of questions for the spirits to answer – as they did.

The following year, he published more than 500 questions, answers and personal

Below: J.H. Pestalozzi presides over the schoolyard. This revolutionary educationalist profoundly influenced the early course of Rivail's life, impressing him with his progressive attitudes. He was one of the first to encourage small children to develop their personalities at the same time as broadening their minds with a formidable range of lessons

Left: the high point of a Victorian seance – the table mysteriously levitates. Rivail approached such phenomena – and the alleged spirit communications – with caution, but came to believe that there was some serious purpose underlying the frivolous and the trite messages commonly received

commentaries under the title *Le livre des ésprits* (translated as *The spirits' book*), which he revised and enlarged three years later. It appeared under the name Allan Kardec, a name from Rivail's Breton ancestry apparently selected by the spirits themselves. So Rivail became Kardec, and by his death in 1869 he had written, or as he preferred to put it 'compiled and set in order', five books and two monographs, insisting that their main content was not his work, but that of numerous 'advanced' spirits communicating through several different mediums. His chief works were: *The spirits' book* (1857 and 1860), *The mediums' book* (1861), *The gospel according to Spiritism* (1864), *Heaven and hell* (1865) and *Genesis* (1867). He also founded, edited and wrote much of the periodical *Revue Spirite*, until his death in 1869.

Despite his ardent belief in the communication of spirits of the dead, Kardec's philosophy was not part of mainstream Spiritualism, but, as he called it, Spiritism. The difference was crucial to followers of both philosophies and set them on very separate paths for the future.

The visible and invisible

The basic premise of Spiritism is that there are two worlds: the visible and the invisible, which contain material and 'incorporeal' beings respectively. Spirit is an actual substance, formed by 'quintessential' matter beyond the reach of our normal five senses, that unites itself with the physical body by means of an intermediary, semi-material 'perispirit' body. At birth, we assume temporary and perishable material forms, and when these are destroyed by physical death, the spirit remains, eventually to return in another incarnation. Our purpose is to evolve towards perfection, and we reincarnate as often as necessary to achieve this aim. We are all the sum of what we have ever been, done or thought in earlier lives, and the whole process, Kardec insists, is far from miraculous or supernatural, but the working out of immutable and natural laws.

Whereas Spiritualism, as Kardec saw it, merely denoted a belief that there was something more to Man than matter, Spiritism concerned 'the relation of the material world with spirits' – actual entities in constant touch with us. Kardec never claimed it to be a new religion, but a rational philosophy based on repeatedly demonstrated fact that restored all religions to their original purpose. It was certainly not intended, as his critics alleged, to replace Christianity. 'The morality of Spiritism is not different from that of Jesus,' he wrote, arguing that just as Jesus's teaching restated that of Moses, so was Spiritism a restatement of basic Christian principles that had become neglected by almost all organised churches. 'Why is it,' he asked, 'that the moral teachings of Christ are so little practised? And why is it that those who rightly proclaim their sublimity are the first to violate the first of His laws, viz., that of *universal charity*?'

Kardec's books form the clearest and most comprehensive survey of the invisible world yet written. They make an interesting comparison with the writings of Emanuel Swedenborg and Andrew Jackson Davis, 'the Seer of Poughkeepsie', whose *Principles of nature* was published in 1847. Although the three men covered much of the same ground, Kardec is the only one who was neither a medium nor a mystic, but a collector and collator of writings by other hands. His own contribution to his books is limited to commentaries on the material received, and in these he comes across as a man of reason and intelligence. As he put it himself, 'I studied the facts with care and perseverance, I co-ordinated them, and deduced the consequences from them.'

Kardec was one of the earliest serious psychical researchers, and he found time to study paranormal phenomena of many kinds all over France. Twenty years before the founding of the Society for Psychical Research, he was publishing detailed accounts, in the *Revue Spirite* and *The mediums' book*, of several excellent cases that are usually overlooked by historians. He wrote at length about the medium Jean Hillaire, the healer Jacob the Zouave, the mass possession of the town of Morzine, and several examples of what we now call poltergeist activity. He corresponded with D.D. Home, whom he much admired, and witnessed plenty of paranormal activity himself, once watching a table weighing 220 pounds (100 kilograms) balance itself at an angle of 45° on one leg. But he was less interested in such displays than in their implications.

Cause and effect

Every intelligent effect, he argued, must have an intelligent cause, and there was more than sufficient evidence for the reality of communication with the 'dead'. But this did not mean everything they said or wrote should be accepted at face value. 'There is no shortage of writers in the invisible world,' he said, 'but as on Earth the good ones are rare.' Some spirits, he noted, 'know less than we on Earth'. It was up to the researcher to be 'critical and logical'.

Kardec died well before the great period of French psychology and early psychiatry, in which pioneers like Janet, Charcot and Bernheim brought a more clinical approach to bear on hitherto unexplained abnormalities of human experience (many of which remain unexplained to this day). It may be argued that, for all his honesty and intelligence, he was simply deceived by clever fraudulent mediums. This seems unlikely, however, for two main reasons. First, the phenomena he reported and the conclusions he reached were essentially the same as those of other researchers, some with impressive scientific qualifications, from Robert Hare in

Above: Andrew Jackson Davis, American visionary and contemporary of Allan Kardec

Above: Adolfo Bezerra de Meneses, the statesman responsible for the spread of Brazilian Spiritism

the USA to Alfred Russel Wallace, and later Sir William Crookes, in Britain, all of whom found their beliefs altered by observation.

Second, as Kardec repeatedly insisted himself, it was what the better-quality spirit messages had to say that was of real value, not the phenomenon itself. The message, in fact, and not the medium was what was important. 'They may laugh at the turning tables,' he wrote, 'but they will never laugh at the philosophy, the knowledge and the charity that shine out from the serious communications.'

Predictably, Kardec was none too popular with the Catholic Church, which placed his work on the *Index librorum prohibitorum* in 1866, but even so he often replied in painstaking detail to criticism. He once thanked a priest for attacking him 'politely, and in more or less correct French', and when a pile of his books were burned in Barcelona in 1861, he merely commented, 'You can burn books, but you cannot burn ideas.'

Practical Spiritism

His books have remained in print in several languages, and his ideas have had considerable impact in many countries, notably in Brazil, where the Spiritist movement soon won respectability chiefly due to the support of the doctor and statesman Adolfo Bezerra de Meneses. Today, opinion polls have estimated over 20 million Brazilians to be practising Spiritists and, mindful of Kardec's insistence on charity as their first duty, they have carried out some of the most impressive social welfare projects to be found anywhere.

Brazil now has large hospitals that combine medical and spiritual treatment, orphanages, training centres for mediums and healers, and public halls where free guidance and healing are given to anybody who asks for it. At one of these, in the centre of São Paulo, 1000 people are attended every day by 200 volunteer mediums. Several million copies of Kardec's books, and of books inspired by them, have been sold, and Kardec's portrait has appeared no less than three times on Brazilian postage stamps.

This unique honour might have embarrassed the man who wrote, in the 'Conclusion' of *The spirits' book*:

What is the special and peculiar work of modern Spiritism? To make a coherent whole of what has hitherto been scattered; to explain, in clear and precise terms, what has hitherto been wrapped up in the language of allegory; to eliminate the products of superstition and ignorance from human belief, leaving only what is real and actual. This is its mission.

The facts of Spiritism, he concluded, had given the death-blow to materialism and 'shown the inevitable results of evil and consequently the necessity of goodness', while as for the future life, this was no longer a 'vague imagining, a mere hope, but a fact'.

Were the catastrophes described in the Bible caused by a near-collision between the Earth and the infant planet Venus? COLIN WILSON examines the amazing theories put forward by Immanuel Velikovsky in the 1940s

ONE DAY IN 1947, a bulky and dog-eared manuscript landed on the desk of an editor in the New York office of the publishing house of Macmillan. It was called *Worlds in collision*, and it looked impressively erudite. Its author, apparently, was a 52-year-old Freudian psychiatrist named Immanuel Velikovsky. But what on earth was a psychiatrist doing writing about planets and comets and the birth of the solar system? Clearly, this was a consideration that had struck other publishers, to judge from the state of the typescript (in fact, it had been rejected more than a dozen times). Nevertheless, the editor who read it was impressed and excited. What this man was saying might be nonsense – but it was fascinating nonsense. He claimed, for example, that biblical miracles such as the parting of the Red Sea had really happened, and were simply due to strange convulsions among the planets.

The editor cautiously recommended it; but Macmillans were not so sure. They were a respectable academic publisher, with a large textbook list; they could not afford to be

Below: the mysterious planet Venus. Until the second millennium BC, Venus was not grouped by astronomers with the other planets: it was described as a threatening comet-like body that was believed to rain down fire on the Earth. This fact led Immanuel Velikovsky (right) to suggest that perhaps Venus was not, in fact, a planet at this period. He claimed it was actually a comet that, coming very close to the Earth, caused many of the catastrophes described in the Bible – the Flood, the plagues of Egypt and the fall of the walls of the city of Jericho

accused of encouraging the lunatic fringe. They decided to compromise, and offered Velikovsky a small advance, and a contract that gave them an option to publish his book – so he could not now sell it elsewhere – but no guarantee that they would in fact do so. But a year later, they decided to go ahead with publication and offer him a more favourable contract.

Who was this erudite psychiatrist? Velikovsky, it seemed, was a Russian Jew, born in Vitebsk in June 1895, who had studied mathematics in Moscow. He went on to study medicine, qualifying in 1921, and

In the comet's tail

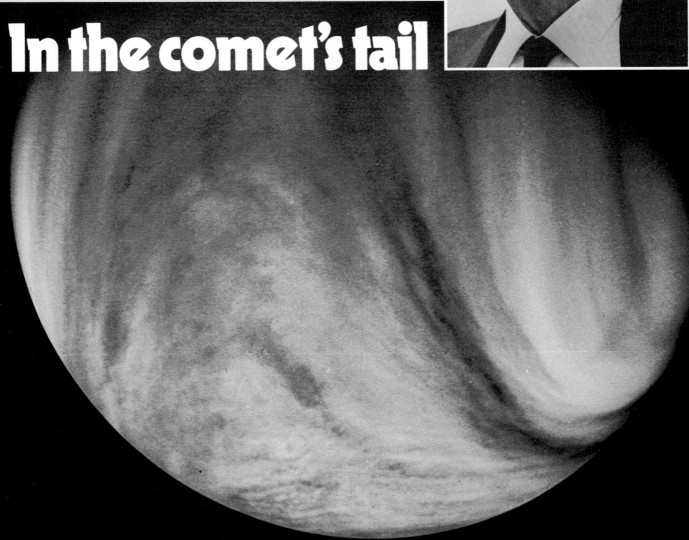

studied psychiatry in Vienna with Freud's pupil Wilhelm Stekel. In 1924, he moved to Palestine and practised there as a psychiatrist, also becoming interested in the archaeology of the land of his forefathers. A reading of Freud's *Moses and monotheism* (1937) electrified him. This book proposed a bold and startling thesis: first, that the great lawgiver Moses was not a Jew, but an Egyptian; second, that he was a follower of the religion of the pharaoh Akhenaten, the king who created a new religion of the Sun-god and who was probably overthrown; third, that Moses fled from Egypt when Akhenaten was dead and imposed the new religion of a single God on the Jews.

Dazzling boldness

Freud's theory, of course, flies in the face of the story related in the Bible. One objection to it is that, according to historians, Moses lived more than a century after the death of Akhenaten; but Freud contested this view, and moved fearlessly into the area of historical research. Dazzled by his boldness, Velikovsky decided to do the same. And he soon reached an even more startling and unorthodox conclusion: that the pharaoh Akhenaten was, in fact, the legendary Oedipus of Greek legend, and that the Oedipus legend arose from the fact that Akhenaten had married his own mother.

Having launched himself into this area of historical research, Velikovsky became fascinated by it. And his study of Moses and Akhenaten soon led him to a conclusion beside which even Freud's heterodox views seemed conservative and timid: that the various events that accompanied the flight of the Jews out of Egypt – the plagues, the crossing of the Red Sea, the destruction of the Egyptian armies by floods, the pillar of cloud by day, the manna that fell from heaven – were the outcome of some great cosmic upheaval. Is it possible, Velikovsky wondered, that there are other records of the catastrophe? At this point, he stumbled on exactly what he was looking for – an obscure ancient papyrus written by an Egyptian sage

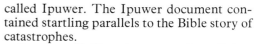

Velikovsky's work was inspired by a book written by his fellow psychiatrist Sigmund Freud, *Moses and monotheism*. Freud suggested that Moses (left) was an Egyptian, not a Jew; that he was a follower of the pharaoh Akhenaten (above), who introduced to Egypt a new monotheistic religion; and that Moses had brought this religion to the Jews. Velikovsky's researches led him to an even more extraordinary conclusion – that Akhenaten, who married his own mother, became the Oedipus of Greek legend (below left)

called Ipuwer. The Ipuwer document contained startling parallels to the Bible story of catastrophes.

In 1939, Velikovsky moved from Palestine to the United States – perhaps because he needed access to great libraries. He spent the next five years building up the evidence for his amazing theory. If there *had* been some tremendous event in the heavens, what could it be? The German Hanns Hörbiger had put forward an off-beat theory that the Earth has had several moons, not just one, and that legendary stories of great catastrophes are racial memories of these moons exploding in the sky and crashing down to Earth. Could this be the answer? Velikovsky studied the records, and decided against it. There was a far more exciting clue. Before

Evidence for the flood

One of the main assumptions of Velikovsky's argument is that the legends of great floods that are found all over the world all, in fact, refer to the same event – a cataclysmic deluge that swept the entire earth.

It is certainly true that flood legends feature in the mythologies of many peoples. The most familiar is the biblical story of Noah and the Flood (illustrated in John Martin's *The assuaging of the waters*, left). Among many similar legends throughout the world is one told by the Chippewa Indians of Ontario, Canada, which links the flood with the end of the last ice age: 'A little mouse nibbled a hole in the leather bag which contained the sun's heat, and the heat poured out over the earth and melted all the snow in an instant. The meltwater kept on rising until even the highest mountains were submerged.'

Does archaeological evidence bear out the idea of a world flood? The most famous piece of evidence is the discovery by Sir Leonard Woolley in 1929 of a 'flood stratum' of clay at his excavations of the city of Ur. But – unfortunately for Velikovsky – there are no such flood deposits at sites even a few miles away, let alone over a widespread area.

the second millennium BC – and even later – the planet Venus was not grouped by astronomers with the other planets. Velikovsky argued that this might mean that Venus might not have behaved like a planet at this time. He believed that, at some time in the past, there was a gigantic explosion inside the planet Jupiter, an explosion that resulted in the expulsion of a huge molten mass that became a comet – later the planet Venus – whose orbit lay close to that of the Earth. The ancient manuscripts Velikovsky studied contained tantalising references to something that sounded like the near collision of a comet with the Earth: there were immense earthquakes, volcanoes erupted, cities were wiped out, whole countries laid waste. And this, Velikovsky came to believe, was the catastrophe described in the Bible.

There was more to the story. There was evidence that, seven centuries later, the same comet wandered a little too close to Mars, and caused the same kind of upheaval in that planet. Mars was dragged out of its orbit, and the Earth was endangered. Again, the surface of our planet endured gigantic convulsions. And the comet, slowed down by its close encounter, settled down to become the planet Venus.

Velikovsky was aware that his theory was, to put it mildly, rather unorthodox. Yet his study of historical documents convinced him it was not pure fantasy. It was simply an amazing discovery that happened to have

Below: Harlow Shapley, an American astronomer well-known for his pioneering work on the structure of galaxies. At first he was sympathetic to Velikovsky's ideas but he later became one of his most bitter critics; at one time he went as far as to say that Velikovsky's theories were 'complete nonsense'

been so far overlooked. Now it was merely a matter of drawing it to the attention of scientists, and awaiting their criticisms and comments. A year before he submitted the typescript to Macmillans, Velikovsky went out of his way to meet the eminent astronomer Harlow Shapley. Shapley had himself put forward a highly controversial theory about the place of our solar system in the Galaxy, and had encountered bitter opposition – he was surely the man to appreciate Velikovsky's theory. Shapley was polite, but said he was too busy to read *Worlds in collision*. He suggested that a colleague, a sociologist named Horace Kallen, should read it first, and see whether he thought it worth bothering about. And Shapley himself promised to try to obtain the spectroscopic analysis of the atmospheres of Mars and Venus that Velikovsky needed.

Kallen read *Worlds in collision*, and was deeply impressed. He told Shapley that it seemed a serious and worthwhile book and that, even if it should prove to be nonsense, it was still a bold and fascinating thesis.

Shapley, however, did not seem to be at all interested. He replied snappily that Velikovsky's conclusions seemed to him to be based on 'incompetent data' – an odd statement, considering that he had not read the book – and withdrew his offer to provide spectroscopic analysis.

In January 1950, *Harper's* magazine contained a long article about a forthcoming

book by Eric Larrabee. It aroused immediate and widespread interest. And Shapley immediately wrote Macmillans a rather curious letter. He had heard, he said, that they had decided not to publish *Worlds in collision* after all, and could only say that he was greatly relieved to hear it. He had discussed it with various scientists, and all were astonished that Macmillan should venture into 'the Black Arts'.

Macmillans replied cautiously that the book was not supposed to be hard science, but was a controversial theory that various scholars ought to know about. This drew an irritable reply from Shapley. Velikovsky, he said, was 'complete nonsense', and when he had introduced himself to Shapley in a New York hotel, Shapley had looked around to see if Velikovsky had a keeper with him. He now thought that *Worlds in collision* was 'quite possibly intellectually fraudulent' – a legpull designed to make money – and if Macmillans insisted on publishing it, they had better be prepared to drop Shapley from their list.

In spite of this, Macmillans went ahead, and *Worlds in collision* appeared on 3 April 1950. Predictably, it climbed like a rocket to the top of the best-sellers lists. There is a vast audience of 'fundamentalists' who are deeply interested in the Bible, and convinced that every word in it is literally true. (It was this same audience that was to make Werner Keller's *Bible as history* a best-seller a few years later in 1956.) Now that it looked as though there might be scientific evidence to support the biblical 'miracles' – including the parting of the Red Sea and the falling of the walls of Jericho – they rushed to buy the book. So did thousands of ordinary, intelligent readers who enjoy an adventure in

According to Velikovsky's theory, the parting of the waters of the Red Sea (above) happened as the Earth was passing through the tail of the comet that later became the planet Venus. The waters parted until the comet and the Earth met with an enormous electrical discharge – then the waves surged together again, drowning the pharaoh's army. Life on Earth might have been wiped out entirely had the comet not dropped food – the manna gathered and eaten by the Jews (right)

speculative thought. Immanuel Velikovsky and his theories had become famous.

But the scientific establishment showed a certain lack of the spirit of intellectual adventure. They seemed to feel that Macmillans had committed some appalling error of taste in issuing the book. One scientist who had read the book in manuscript – Gordon Atwater, chairman of the astronomy department at New York's Museum of Natural History – was sacked when he published a review urging that scientists ought to be open-minded about the book. James Putnam, the editor who had decided to publish *Worlds in collision*, was dismissed from Macmillans. Respectable professors deluged Macmillans with letters threatening to boycott their textbooks if *Worlds in collision* was not withdrawn. Macmillans gave in under this pressure and *Worlds in collision* was

Left: a photograph of the surface of Jupiter, taken by *Voyager I* in 1979. Could it really be, as Velikovsky argued, that Venus started life as a comet that erupted from Jupiter?

passed on to the Doubleday company, who had no profitable textbook department to worry about. But this did nothing to stop the hue and cry. *Worlds in collision* went on selling steadily, and scientists seemed to be driven to a frenzy by its success. Fred Whipple, Shapley's successor at the Harvard Observatory, wrote to Doubleday telling them that he wanted to take his own book *Earth, Moon and planets* off their list if they persisted in publishing *Worlds in collision*. Fortunately, they ignored this blackmail. Twenty years later, in *The Village Voice*, Whipple published another letter denying that he had ever tried to dissuade Doubleday from taking Velikovsky off their list. (Both letters can be found in *Velikovsky reconsidered*, by Norman Storer.)

Velikovsky himself was rather bewildered by all this controversy. He had expected disagreement, not persecution. Everyone who knew him was aware that he was a serious scholar, not a crank or publicity seeker. Like any open-minded scientist, he was quite willing to admit that he might well be wrong. However, the historical records had shown clearly that *something* had taken place. Why couldn't the scientists acknowledge that, and *then* criticise his ideas?

Clearly, there was only one thing to do: gather more evidence, and go on presenting it until someone was forced to discuss it seriously. So Velikovsky returned to his reference books.

Right: the falling down of the walls of Jericho. Velikovsky believed that the young planet Venus, while still a comet, caused the parting of the waters of the Red Sea; 50 years later it returned, fortuitously just in time to help Joshua capture the city of Jericho

Catastrophe and controversy

Velikovsky's work was greeted with derision by his opponents; his theory of 'cataclysmic evolution' was dismissed as proof of his intellectual irresponsibility. But modern research supports many of his most startling conclusions

THE STORY OF THE PUBLICATION of Velikovsky's *Worlds in collision* – and the subsequent attempts to suppress it – is one of the sorriest chapters in the history of ideas. In his book *Scientists confront Velikovsky*, the sociologist Norman Storer does his best to excuse the attitude of the scientists. He points out that 1950 was in many ways a bad year, with the Cold War at its chilliest, and reactionary forces – exemplified by Senator Joe McCarthy's 'non-American activities' campaign – steadily gathering strength. Storer pleads disarmingly for the scientists:

> If we add to this the fact that Velikovsky could be only marginally distinguished from the myriad of eccentrics who have always assailed science, perhaps the initial response to his work can be understood.

Plausible as this is, however, it fails to explain the gibbering rage with which respected scientists greeted the book, or their determined efforts to suppress it. It is no excuse to say that the scientific community was itself a little paranoid at the time.

To be fair, it is true that Velikovsky's basic thesis *sounds* lunatic. He is asking us to believe that, sometime before 1500 BC, a comet erupted out of Jupiter. As far as we know, comets do *not* erupt out of planets. He is asking us to believe that this comet came close to the Earth at the time Moses was trying to persuade Pharaoh to let the Israelites out of Egypt and that, as the Earth passed through the comet's tail, Egypt was smitten with the plagues described in the Bible – falling blood, locusts and so on, and the death of all the firstborn. He is asking us to believe that, as the centre of the comet came closer to the Earth, the waters of the Red Sea rose until the two bodies met, when there was an almighty electrical discharge and the waters fell again – conveniently for the Israelites, who walked across the Red Sea dry-shod when the waters were sucked back, while the pursuing Egyptians were drowned when the waters were released again. Life on Earth might have become extinct were it not for the fact that the comet also dropped a kind of food in the form of carbohydrates – manna – that kept the survivors alive. Fifty years later, the comet returned just as Joshua was leading the Israelites into the Promised Land, and the walls of Jericho collapsed in the resultant earthquake.

Most reasonable people feel that Velikovsky's hypotheses go too far. In a sense, Velikovsky is a true Freudian in that

Right: a computer-enhanced photograph of the 3-million-mile (5-million-kilometre) tail of Comet Kohoutek, taken by *Skylab* in 1973. Velikovsky believed that the catastrophes described in the Bible – such as the plagues that afflicted Egypt (above right) – occurred when the Earth passed through the tail of a comet that later became the planet Venus

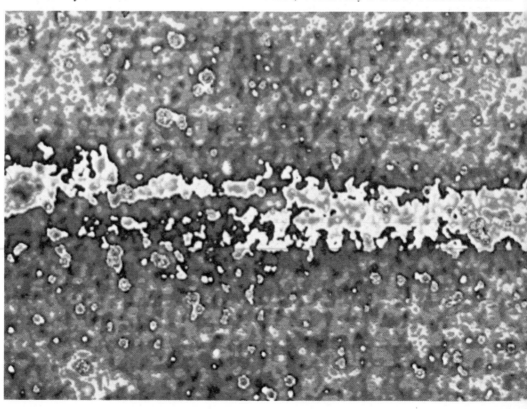

he cannot resist seeing all the facts he comes across in terms of his theory – as Freud, for example, saw just about every genius in history as an illustration of the Oedipus complex. But the fact remains that Velikovsky has presented a case to be answered.

While the controversy over *Worlds in collision* was still raging, Velikovsky moved from New York to Princeton, and began to spend his days in the library of the Princeton Department of Geology. He was studying the material on tremendous convulsions that have distorted the surface of our Earth at remote epochs in the past. In doing so, he was aware that he was reviving a theory that had been discredited in the 19th century. It was called catastrophism, and it was an attempt to explain such mysteries as fossil dinosaurs. How had these species come to vanish? The answer, according to eminent scientists like Georges Cuvier (1769–1832), was that a series of violent catastrophes had wiped out these species, so nature had had to start from scratch again. Lyell's *Principles of geology* and Darwin's *Origin of species* destroyed the catastrophe theory by showing that our Earth is in fact thousands of millions of years old – not a few thousand, as had been assumed – and that the dinosaurs became extinct over a long period by the gradual process of natural selection.

Or *did* they? One of the unexplained facts of prehistory is that dinosaurs vanished quite suddenly – overnight, as it were. They had

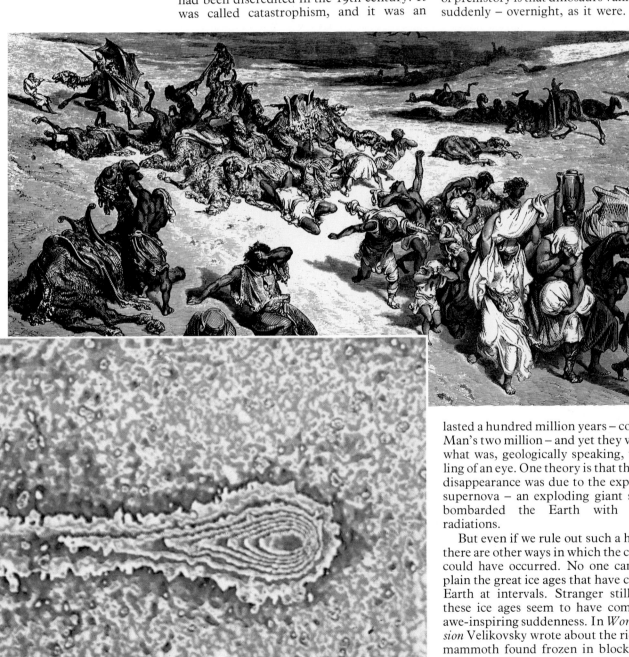

lasted a hundred million years – compared to Man's two million – and yet they vanished in what was, geologically speaking, the twinkling of an eye. One theory is that their sudden disappearance was due to the explosion of a supernova – an exploding giant star – that bombarded the Earth with poisonous radiations.

But even if we rule out such a hypothesis, there are other ways in which the catastrophe could have occurred. No one can fully explain the great ice ages that have covered the Earth at intervals. Stranger still, some of these ice ages seem to have come on with awe-inspiring suddenness. In *Worlds in collision* Velikovsky wrote about the riddle of the mammoth found frozen in blocks of ice in a river in Siberia in 1799. He might have gone on to mention the Berezovka mammoth, discovered in Siberia around the turn of the century; the meat was still as edible as quick-frozen steak, and there were grasses

Darwin's theory of evolution is highly questionable. Immense biological changes *do* occur in sudden leaps. Geneticists are busy trying to understand the mechanism by which these occur, and they may find satisfactory explanations that do not require the hypothesis of outside intervention. Meanwhile, it is interesting to see that Velikovsky's heterodox theory begins to look more like a genuine scientific inspiration.

It was unfortunate for Velikovsky that, by the time *Earth in upheaval* appeared in 1956, the general public had largely lost interest in the controversy. By this time, he had published the first volume of his 'revised chronology of ancient history', *Ages in chaos* (1952), and most ordinary readers must have found this work confusing and boring – it is a

The wall paintings at Deir el-Bahri (above left) show the Egyptian Queen Hatshepsut's journey to the mysterious land of Punt. Velikovsky suggests that the paintings show the Queen on her way to Jerusalem to visit King Solomon – and that Hatshepsut was actually the Queen of Sheba (left, in an illustration from a 15th-century manuscript). Hatshepsut is believed to have lived some centuries before Solomon – but Velikovsky boldly argues that she actually lived some 600 years later than is assumed

and fresh buttercups in its stomach. Velikovsky consulted a quick-freezing firm, who admitted that it would have no idea of how to go about freezing a whole mammoth so that the flesh remained edible after thousands of years. It takes 30 minutes to quick-freeze a mere side of beef. But a creature the size of a mammoth – covered with hair – could not be penetrated by cold in less than days, and the stomach would have had time to start decomposing. This had not happened in the case of the Berezovka mammoth. According to Velikovsky, some sudden catastrophe must have brought the temperature close to absolute zero, and kept it there, to freeze a mammoth through and through. One way in which this could have happened was for volcanoes to have shot out vast quantities of gas and dust into the atmosphere; howling gales would have built up cold fronts, causing huge clouds of icy snow. Such a freezing cloud, encountering a patch of still, warm air – in a protected valley – would descend literally like a ton of bricks. Any mammoths in the valley would be quick-frozen to death.

Cataclysmic evolution

It was ancient catastrophes that Velikovsky proceeded to study at Princeton, and the result was his most readable and fascinating book *Earth in upheaval*. In this book, published in 1955, we can glimpse some of the daring intuition that makes Velikovsky's thought so exciting to follow. After discussing Darwin's theory of evolution, he raises serious doubts about its adequacy, and suggests a theory of 'cataclysmic evolution', in which new species might appear by mutation of genes. At that time, every good biologist in the world was a Darwinian, and Velikovsky's 'cataclysmic evolution' was cited as evidence of his intellectual irresponsibility. Yet now biologists have come to recognise that

Below: the head and leg of a young mammoth found in the Alaskan permafrost. Velikovsky believed that the sudden disappearance of the mammoths could be explained only by a catastrophe that caused a drastic drop in temperature

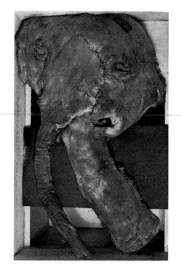

lengthy comparison of various dates in Egyptian and Jewish history, together with an attempt to show that historians have got it all wrong. Even for the intelligent layman, the question of whether Queen Hatshepsut of Egypt was the same person as the Queen of Sheba is scarcely a vital issue.

There was also the fact that *Worlds in collision* had been over-exposed. The mass onslaught on Velikovsky had given readers the impression that his theories had been totally discredited, while the titles of his books – *Worlds in collision*, *Ages in chaos*, *Earth in upheaval* – gave rise to the suspicion that he was a sensationalist. What happened can be compared to the events that followed the publication of *The third eye* by T. Lobsang Rampa when its author was revealed to be an Englishman using a Tibetan pseudonym. Despite his assurances that he was actually the reincarnation of a Tibetan monk, only the faithful stayed around to listen to the sequel. Fortunately, in Velikovsky's case, the 'faithful' finally succeeded in having the whole affair reopened.

A fair hearing

Despite blistering criticism, Velikovsky continued to elaborate on his revolutionary theories. Many of his results have been confirmed by subsequent research – even if his reasoning has often been shown to be wildly off course.

TWO YEARS AFTER THE PUBLICATION of *Worlds in collision*, there appeared in the United States a highly readable and amusing volume called *In the name of science* – later republished as *Fads and fallacies in the name of science* – by Martin Gardner, mathematical correspondent of *Scientific American*. It consisted of a series of lively and incisive accounts of many celebrated 'crank theories', ranging from those of the Flat Earth Society to Wilhelm Reich's orgone box. Gardner's comments on Velikovsky's work are typically scathing. He writes:

Dr Velikovsky is an almost perfect textbook example of the pseudo-

Below: the seventh biblical plague of Egypt – fire and hail – in a painting by John Martin. Scientists poured scorn on Velikovsky's theory that this and many other ancient disasters were caused by the near-collision of the Earth with a comet. But could Velikovsky's theory nevertheless have been right?

scientist, self taught in the subjects in which he does most of the speculation, working in total isolation from fellow scientists, motivated by a strong compulsion to defend dogmas held for other than scientific reasons, and with an unshakeable conviction in the revolutionary value of his work and the blindness of his critics.

Gardner goes on to complain that most of Velikovsky's 'evidence' consists of legends that are supposed to be memories of ancient catastrophes. As to Velikovsky's painstaking attempt to justify his new chronology of ancient history, Gardner dismisses it with a mere mention: 'Nor need we be concerned with the doctor's projected two volume revision of the ancient history of the East. The first half of this fantasy, *Ages in chaos*, was published in 1952.'

This may seem to fall a little short of a thoroughgoing criticism. But Gardner's account of Velikovsky reveals the immense difficulty of trying to arrive at a balanced assessment of this brilliant and exasperating polymath. It *does* sound preposterous to argue that it was a comet thrown off by Jupiter that caused the various plagues that devastated Egypt in the time of Moses, that caused the parting of the Red Sea to let the Israelites cross dry-shod, that made the walls

of Jericho fall down and that, many centuries later, caused the famous destruction of the armies of Sennacherib, the Assyrian king who dared attack the cities of Judah. It just sounds too good to be true. We may feel that Gardner has no right to dismiss *Ages in chaos* as a fantasy when his text makes it clear that he has not read it. Yet, on the whole, his sheer exasperation is understandable. And so is that of the other scientists who attacked Velikovsky tooth and nail.

Yet as soon as we turn to Velikovsky's own life-work, particularly to the immense *Ages in chaos* series (which remained incomplete, in three fat volumes, at Velikovsky's death in November 1979), it becomes possible to see why the attacks on him were so vitriolic. He is one of those headstrong men who get one extraordinary inspiration, and spend a lifetime following it through. What we need to grasp first of all is that Velikovsky was an ardent follower of Freud, whose *Moses and monotheism* started him on his lifelong quest into the history of the Jews. Freud himself was a brilliant and wrongheaded man of genius who built up an immense theory about the sexual origin of all neuroses on a few dubious case histories, and went on to interpret all other cases in its light; it was not until many years after his death that psychologists dared to state openly that much of his work hardly deserves to be called science.

Like Freud, Velikovsky seemed to find nothing but confirmation of his theories in everything he read. Ancient texts describe Venus as a threatening and erratic planet-deity that was said to rain down fire on the Earth. Could that mean that Venus was

What happened in the six centuries between the destruction of Crete (above, the Great Staircase at Knossos) and the emergence of the new Greece (below, an Attic vase)? Velikovsky boldly argued that the generally accepted time-scale of the ancient world was 'out' by some 600 years

actually the agent of past catastrophes, and that it was a comet-like body before it settled down into its present planetary orbit? And could the comet have caused the catastrophes described in the Bible?

Anyone who takes the smallest interest in ancient history will know that there are some intriguing mysteries that have never been cleared up. For example, why did the Minoan civilisation of ancient Crete come to an abrupt end round about 1500 BC? There is

one intriguing possibility. A giant volcano on the island of Santorini, to the north of Crete, exploded like a huge hydrogen bomb around this time. Some writers have suggested that Santorini was actually the mythical (and corrupt) continent of Atlantis; others claim that the explosion destroyed the Minoan civilisation. It certainly could have done, but there is one major objection: Phaistos, in southern Crete, was destroyed at the same time, and even the biggest tidal wave could not wash over the range of high mountains in between. Velikovsky's hypothesis of the near-miss with the comet Venus would explain it much better.

But then, Velikovsky made the mistake of mentioning Atlantis in his work, and this was enough to make most scientists dismiss him as a member of the lunatic fringe.

There was another reason for the failure to take Velikovsky seriously. In studying the history of the Middle East, as revealed in its documents and legends, Velikovsky came to feel that the historians had got many of the dates wrong. Freud (in *Moses and monotheism*) advanced the heterodox view that the exodus of the Jews from Egypt occurred in the reign of the pharaoh Akhenaten, the heretic who founded a new religion of Sun-worship and was probably murdered for his pains; Freud thought that Moses was a disciple of Akhenaten who carried the new religion among the Jews. But Velikovsky's studies led him to reject Freud's theory completely. One of the puzzles about the ancient history of the Mediterranean area is what happened between the destruction of ancient Crete and the emergence of the new

Above: the psychoanalyst Sigmund Freud (1856–1939), whose work on ancient Jewish history inspired Velikovsky's own researches

Below: a relief showing the siege of the Israelite city of Lachish by the armies of the Assyrian king Sennacherib, in about 700 BC. Velikovsky believed that the comet that caused the biblical plagues of Egypt returned and destroyed the armies of Sennacherib

Greece of Homer and – later – Socrates. Were they just blank years? Opting, as usual, for the controversial solution, Velikovsky decided that ancient history was all wrong, and that many important events happened 600 years later than assumed – so closing this huge time-gap. In order to prove this, he undertook a vast work comparing the chronologies of Egypt, Israel, Assyria and Babylonia. The resulting *Ages in chaos* is a work that will be studied only by the most devoted followers; others will find it almost unreadable.

A good example is the problem of the so-called 'Venus tablets of Ammizaduga'. The tablets were found at the mound of Kuyunjik, the site of ancient Nineveh, among the other documents of the enormous library of King Ashurbanipal. They list observations of the planet Venus that are strangely at odds with calculations based on the present movements of the planets. An early commentator wrote: 'Obviously, the days of the month have been mixed up. As the impossible intervals show, the months are wrong'; 'the observations were defective', said another; but Velikovsky disagreed.

Rogue planet

Velikovsky presented the observations as evidence that Venus had moved irregularly at some point in Babylonian history. At a meeting of the American Association for the Advancement of Science held in 1974 with the intent of refuting Velikovsky's theories once and for all, the mathematician Peter Huber claimed that the tablets – with certain 'corrections' – showed that Venus travelled

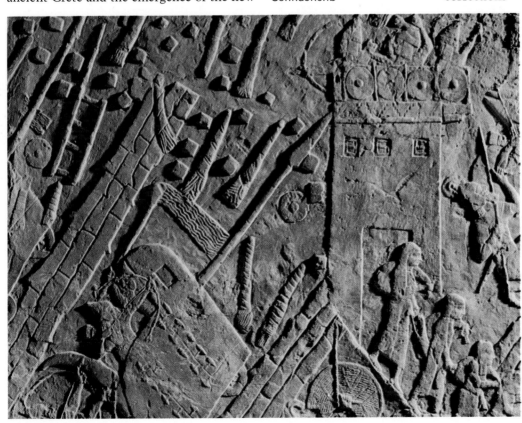

in the same regular orbit that it does today. However, two other scholars, Professor Lynn Rose, a specialist in ancient philosophy and astronomy, and Raymond Vaughan, an optics expert, have shown that, by taking the data on the tablets at face value, and allowing for only a few scribal errors, they can be interpreted to indicate a plausible orbit for Venus different from the one it holds today. Huber himself admitted that, to make the data on the tablets fit a normal orbit, one has to assume that 30 per cent of the entries were scribal errors. Rose and Vaughan put the figure for such adjustments nearer to 60 per cent. So that round, at least, seems to go to Velikovsky.

Another example shows him to have been right again. Velikovsky's theory of the upheaval in our solar system involved the notion of powerful electromagnetic forces; scientists said there was no evidence for such forces. But the discovery of the Van Allan belts of electromagnetic radiation around the Earth in the early 1960s made it clear that Velikovsky was right again.

Over many years, Velikovsky's defenders fought doggedly to try to obtain justice. And, because most people are fair-minded, and because many of the attacks on Velikovsky had been – in Martin Gardner's own words about Velikovsky himself – 'motivated by a strong compulsion to defend dogmas for other than scientific reasons', these attempts gradually achieved success. By the time of his death in 1979, Velikovsky was widely recognised as a courageous and brilliant scholar whose chief offence was the immense range of his intellectual curiosity. In 1972 an

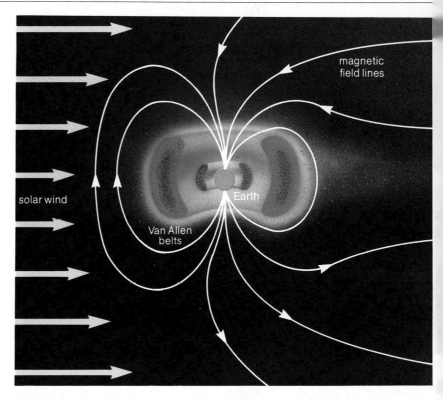

Above: the Van Allan belts of electromagnetic radiation, which surround the Earth like a pair of giant doughnuts. Their discovery in 1958 seemed to vindicate Velikovsky's belief that upheavals in our solar system were caused by electromagnetic forces

American magazine called *Pensée* devoted itself to a comprehensive 'reconsideration' of Velikovsky that ran through many issues. Excerpts have subsequently been published in book form as *Velikovsky reconsidered*. A book called *The Velikovsky affair* (1966) had already revealed just how underhand had been some of the methods used to brand him as a crank. For the remaining years of his life, Velikovsky was enthusiastically received as a lecturer at universities, and made many appearances on American television.

Did he convince the public that his catastrophe theory was correct? The answer must be no. He convinced them only that he was no crank, but a man of seriousness and integrity, whose theories deserved careful attention and research.

And *are* his views correct? One is inclined to doubt it. One can study Velikovsky with absorption, from the amazing geological claims of *Earth in upheaval* to the complex historical arguments of *Ramses the second and his time*. And, on the whole, one still sympathises with Martin Gardner's criticisms. While many scientists are happy to admit that global catastrophes and major disturbances in the solar system may have occurred millions of years ago, they believe the geological records of the Earth and the Moon do not support the idea of Velikovskian upheavals only a few thousand years ago. For all his vast amount of 'evidence', Velikovsky has not *proved* that a comet shot out of Jupiter, destroyed the Egyptian armies and the walls of Jericho, and became Venus. But if – unlikely as it may seem today – he is one day proved to be correct, his work will have been an astonishing example of pure scientific inspiration.

The birth of Venus

Velikovsky's theories enabled him to make a number of predictions about Venus. Scientists were sceptical when he claimed that Venus must rotate in the opposite direction to the other inner planets, that it must have a massive atmosphere, and that its surface temperature must be very high – because, he believed, it had not yet lost all the heat of its explosive departure from Jupiter. But the space probes of the 1970s provided spectacular confirmation of his ideas.

However, these successes were far from vindicating Velikovsky's theory as a whole. The reasoning that led him to his conclusions is often highly dubious – and there are serious grounds for doubting the physical possibility of his claims. Astronomers are agreed that comets do *not* erupt out of planets – and neither can they settle down to become planets. And, in the 2500 years that have passed since, Velikovsky claimed, the comet caused the destruction of the armies of Sennacherib, it could not possibly have settled down into the almost circular orbit Venus has today.

Flash of inspiration

Nikola Tesla, neglected pioneer of electrical energy,
tapped the elemental forces of the planet in his search
for ways to transmit power without wires. NEIL POWELL
relates the history of a prolific inventor whose work
may yet revolutionise the modern world

DURING THE NIGHT of 7 January 1943, an 86-year-old man died alone in his room in the New Yorker Hotel in Manhattan. Before his body was removed to Campbell's Funeral Parlor at 81st Street and Madison Avenue, agents from the Federal Bureau of Investigation entered his room, opened the small safe that he kept there, and took all the papers that it contained, on the grounds that they might contain details of an important secret weapon.

The man was Nikola Tesla, an electrical

Nikola Tesla, a brilliant inventor and a profound scientist, and one of the few people who have refused the offer of a Nobel prize. Among many other remarkable devices he invented the alternating current generator

engineer whose genius rivalled that of Edison. He has been strangely forgotten, except in the country of his birth, although his name lives on in the Tesla coil, an invention that exploits some of the more bizarre properties of electrical current discovered by Tesla. But this scarcely represents the scope of his wide-ranging scientific achievements.

He was born at midnight on 9 July 1856, in Smiljan, at that time part of the Austro-Hungarian empire, but now in Yugoslavia. It is said that he was accused of cheating at school because he would give the answer to a mathematical question incredibly quickly. Indeed, from his earliest years until the end of his life, Tesla claimed that all his understanding of the complex engineering problems to which he devoted his attention came to him in flashes of intuition.

An interview published in the American magazine *The World* on 22 August 1894 gives us a striking picture of Nikola Tesla at the height of his powers:

He has eyes set very far back in his head. They are rather light. I asked him how he could have such light eyes and be a Slav. He told me that his eyes were once much darker, but that using his mind a great deal had made them many shades lighter. I have often heard it said that using the brain makes the eyes lighter in color. Tesla's confirmation of the theory through his personal experience is important.

He is very thin, is more than six feet [1.8 metres] tall, and weighs less than 140 pounds [64 kilograms]. He has very big hands. His thumbs are remarkably big, even for such big hands. They are extraordinarily big. The thumb is the intellectual part of the hand. The apes have very small thumbs. Study them and you will notice this.

Nikola Tesla has a head that spreads out at the top like a fan. His head is shaped like a wedge. His chin is pointed as an ice-pick. His mouth is too small. His chin, though not weak, is not strong enough. His face cannot be studied and judged like the faces of other men, for he is not a worker in practical fields. He lives his life up in the top of his head, where ideas are born, and up there he has plenty of room. His hair is jet black and curly. He stoops – most men do when they have no peacock blood in them. He lives inside of himself. He takes a profound interest in his own work. He has that supply of self-love and self-confidence which usually goes with success. And he differs from most of the men who are written and talked about in the fact that he has something to tell.

Migration to America

And Tesla certainly had something to tell. He had arrived in New York in 1884, his capital four cents, and his baggage comprising some technical articles that he had written in Belgrade and Paris, a book of poems that he had composed, and some calculations that he had made for the design of a flying machine. But in his head he had all the details of the polyphase alternating current generator, which was to become the basis of the Niagara Falls hydroelectric power installation in 1895 and has since become the standard for industrial machinery. As Lord Kelvin, the distinguished British scientist, put it: 'Tesla has contributed more to electrical science than any man up to his time.'

Soon after his arrival in New York, Tesla was employed by Edison, for whom he designed 24 types of dynamo. But the two men did not hit it off, and in April 1887 Tesla was set up in his own laboratory. Here he rapidly showed that his AC system was much superior to Edison's DC system, and in little

Left: Nikola Tesla in 1879, at the age of 23. Still a student, he had produced many speculative proposals for daring inventions, but had as yet no practical achievements to show

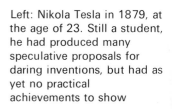

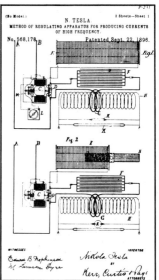

over a year he had been granted no less than 30 important patents.

In the next 20 years, Tesla made an astounding number of discoveries in the field of electrical and radio engineering. Unhappily, due to a succession of accidents in which many of his writings were destroyed, and to the neglect that his name has suffered, it is not always possible to determine the date at which many of his discoveries were made, and so he is seldom credited as a pioneer. There is no doubt, nevertheless, that he, not Marconi, was the discoverer of the tuned circuit upon which radio is based, a fact

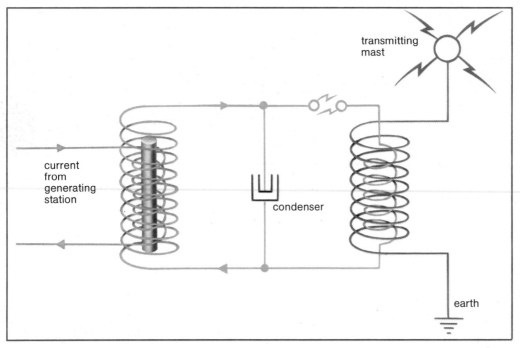

Above: part of Tesla's application for a US patent on the device now known as a 'Tesla coil'. It converts low-voltage direct current into alternating current of very high voltage, which, as Tesla stated in the application, could be used to power fluorescent lamps or produce 'Roentgen shadows' (x-ray images)

Left: the circuits used at Colorado Springs. A low-voltage AC current (blue) was amplified by a giant modified Tesla coil (green). The voltage was still further boosted in the final circuit, through which current was drawn from the ground and discharged from the transmitting mast

Unlike Marconi, however, Tesla was concerned with the transmission not only of minute quantities of energy in the form of radio signals but also of huge amounts of electrical energy for domestic and industrial use. In 1899 he succeeded in pumping power into the atmosphere equivalent to many millions of watts with an immense coil generating some 10 million volts.

The experimental installation that Tesla constructed at Colorado Springs was a barn-shaped building nearly 100 feet (30 metres) square. From the centre of the roof a skeletal tower supported a mast nearly 200 feet (60 metres) high on top of which was mounted a copper ball some 3 feet (90 centimetres) in diameter. Inside the building was a circular enclosure like a fence, some 75 feet (23 metres) in diameter, on which was wound the primary coil of his transmitter; the secondary coil was about 10 feet (3 metres) in diameter, and was connected to the mast.

Circuits in tune

The principle behind the tuned resonant circuit is very like that of the child's swing. A small push starts the swing, and the same small push, applied at the right moment, soon has the swing moving high and wide. In the same way, a succession of electrical pulses, applied with the correct frequency to the primary coil, will produce highly magnified pulses in the secondary coil.

These pulses in the mast connected to Tesla's secondary coil would generate high-frequency radio waves that would travel to the far side of the globe and then return. If they were precisely tuned to the natural frequency of oscillation of electrical currents in the Earth, they would, on their return, exactly reinforce the voltage pulses in the mast, and boost the current that was drawn from the Earth. An ever-increasing current

determined by the US Supreme Court only in the year of his death. It is probable, also, that he was the first to observe cathode rays and x-rays, ultraviolet radiation, and the therapeutic effects upon the human body of high-frequency currents. He was the first to design the fore-runner of the fluorescent lighting tube, and he may well have developed a laser-like device.

In 1912 Tesla refused the nomination for the Nobel prize in physics; it was said that he felt that he should have received it in 1909 in place of Marconi. Certainly, as early as 1898, he had demonstrated a radio-controlled boat in Madison Square Garden, New York, and in 1899 he built a powerful transmitting station at Colorado Springs, situated on a plateau in the foothills of the Rockies.

Above: a discharge of millions of volts at Colorado Springs. It was not Tesla's practice to use these artificial lightning strokes as reading lamps, as this picture suggests: he was photographed with flash powder and then moved to a safe distance while the current flowed and the film was re-exposed

Below: Madison Square Garden, New York, where Tesla's demonstration of a radio-controlled boat enthralled spectators in 1898

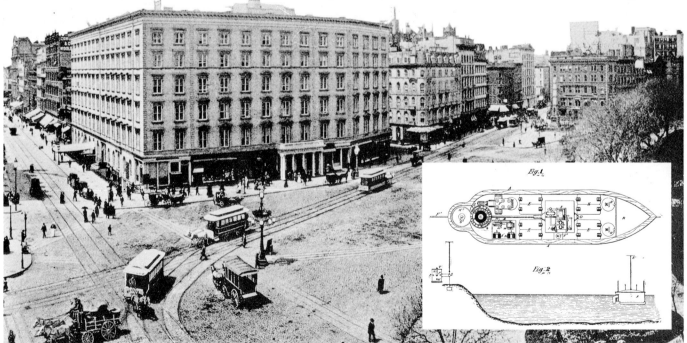

would surge through the apparatus. The entire planet would be used as a further 'secondary circuit' to amplify the current.

The story of how Tesla, 'properly attired in cutaway coat and black derby hat for the auspicious occasion', put his apparatus into operation is dramatically told in John J. O'Neill's *Prodigal genius*. While Tesla watched the top of the mast from outside the building, his assistant Czito stood apprehensively by the controls within. When he closed the switch the secondary coil was surrounded by a halo of electrical fire, sparks crackled through every part of the building, and there came a sharp snap from high overhead.

Now it was followed by a tremendous upsurge of sound. The crackling from the coil swelled into a crescendo . . . the original staccato snap was followed by a sharper one. . . . They came closer together like the rattle of a machine gun. The bang high in the air became tremendously louder; it was now the roar of a cannon, with the discharges rapidly following each other as if a gigantic artillery battle was taking place over the building. . . . There was a strange ghostly blue light in the great barnlike structure. The coils were flaming with masses of fiery hair. Everything in the building was spouting needles of flame. . . .

Outside, Tesla stood entranced. From the copper ball on top of the mast, bolts of lightning were shooting out: fingers of fire nearly 135 feet (40 metres) in length.

Testing to destruction

Suddenly the man-made lightning ceased. Tesla hurried back into his laboratory, protesting to Czito that he had given no orders to stop the experiment. But Czito pointed silently to his control dials, which showed that the power supply had failed. The experiment had completely burnt out the generating system of the Colorado Springs Electric Company.

Fortunately, the company's generator was one of Tesla's own design, and within a week he had it operating again. Some of the implications of the results he obtained from his experiments were indicated in a paper he wrote the following year.

That communication without wires to any point of the globe is practical with such apparatus would need no demonstration, but through a discovery I made I obtained absolute certitude. Popularly explained it is exactly this: When we raise the voice and hear an echo in reply, we know that the sound of the voice must have reached a distant wall, or boundary, and must have been reflected from the same. Exactly as the sound, so an electrical wave is reflected, and the same evidence which is afforded by an echo is offered by an

electrical phenomenon known as a 'stationary' wave – that is, a wave with fixed nodal and ventral regions. Instead of sending sound vibrations toward a distant wall, I have sent electrical vibrations toward the remote boundaries of the earth, and instead of the wall the earth has replied. In place of an echo I have obtained a stationary electrical wave . . . reflected from afar.

A standard demonstration of the effects of the Tesla coil is to cause an electric light bulb to burn brightly without any connection to an electrical supply. With his giant Colorado Springs installation, Tesla was able to light 200 of Edison's incandescent lamps at a

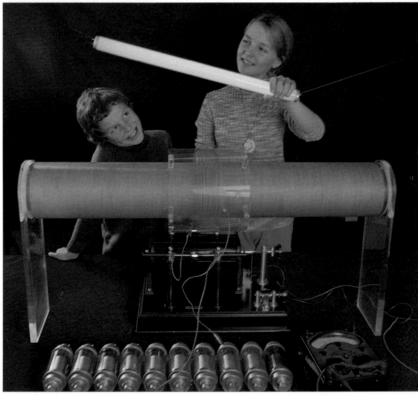

Top: Tesla photographed by the light of a fluorescent lamp of his own invention. High-frequency power is fed to the lamp through wires hidden on Tesla's body. Invisible ultraviolet radiation is produced by low-pressure gas in the lamp and causes a coating on the inside surface to glow. This principle is used in modern fluorescent lighting, with smaller voltages and frequencies

Above: a modern demonstration of Tesla's ideas. The fluorescent tube is being energised by radio-frequency waves from the large Tesla coil, without connecting wires

distance of 25 miles (40 kilometres).

Seventy-eight years later, the London *Evening Standard* reported that some remarkable electrical storms had been taking place over Canada, and that Tesla's last surviving assistant, Arthur Matthews, had been intensively interrogated by an unnamed Russian electrical engineer. Shortly afterward, the same newspaper reported that Major-General George Keegan, former head of US Air Force Intelligence, had publicly voiced his apprehension that the Russians possessed a 'particle gun' capable of detonating ballistic missiles in flight.

These events were linked to the work of Tesla. For it seemed that the principles that had enabled him to transmit energy to distant places and to tap the energies of the Earth were now being harnessed for war.

Tesla's brave new world

Towards the end of his life, Nikola Tesla left hints that he had devised a weapon of unprecedented power and precision.

RETURNING FROM THE GIANT electrical transmitting station he had built at Colorado Springs in 1900, Nikola Tesla embarked upon an even more ambitious project, his so-called 'World System' – a way of using the Earth's natural 'electrical vibrations' to provide universal and inexpensive electrical power. With the financial support of railroad magnate J.P. Morgan, he began the construction of an enormous broadcasting complex on a 2000-acre (800-hectare) estate known as Wardencliff, on Long Island some 60 miles (100 kilometres) from New York. A skeletal wooden tower some 154 feet (45 metres) high was erected, on which Tesla proposed to mount a giant copper electrode 100 feet (30 metres) in diameter, shaped like a huge doughnut with a tube diameter of 20 feet (6 metres).

But somehow, things began to go wrong. There was never enough money, and although the tower stood for 12 years until it was demolished during the First World War as a defence risk, the whole scheme came to nothing. And of the associated project, the industrial 'city beautiful' that he had envisaged with his architect friend Stanford White, there was no sign.

From that time on, Tesla seems to have been a spent force. He was never destitute, he never starved; but, while other scientists and engineers developed the practical applications of ideas for which he could claim the original idea, he found few opportunities to advance his own theories. Indeed, as he grew older, he seemed to lose touch with the scientific community, and increasingly made dogmatic assertions that conflicted with the

Above: a shower of glowing droplets flies from the point of impact of a ruby laser beam on a metallic surface. Military scientists are working on missile-destroying lasers

Left: Tesla in about 1910, surrounded by a battery of sophisticated equipment

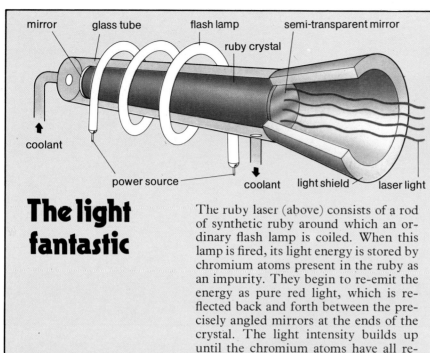

mirror   glass tube   flash lamp   semi-transparent mirror

ruby crystal

coolant

power source   coolant   light shield   laser light

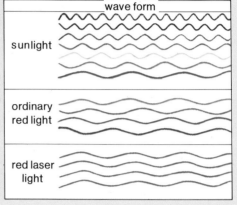

wave form

sunlight

ordinary red light

red laser light

The light fantastic

The ruby laser (above) consists of a rod of synthetic ruby around which an ordinary flash lamp is coiled. When this lamp is fired, its light energy is stored by chromium atoms present in the ruby as an impurity. They begin to re-emit the energy as pure red light, which is reflected back and forth between the precisely angled mirrors at the ends of the crystal. The light intensity builds up until the chromium atoms have all released their energy. The light gradually 'leaks' out through one of the end mirrors, which is semi-transparent, and emerges as a brief pulse of red light.

White light, such as sunlight (below), is a mixture of light of all wavelengths, each wavelength corresponding to a particular colour. Light of even the purest colour obtained from sources other than lasers has a 'spread' of wavelengths; the waves are also out of phase – they are not 'in step'. Laser light, by contrast, is of a single precise wavelength, its waves are in phase, and it can be extremely intense for short periods.

way in which physics was going.

For instance, he could not be persuaded to accept the modern picture of the discrete structure of the atom, and the idea of 'smashing the atom' was to him inconceivable. He accepted the existence of atoms as the indivisible 'billiard balls' of Victorian physics, and he accepted the idea of the independent existence of the electron, but he could not reconcile one concept with the other. As a result of his experiments with extremely long-wave, high-energy electrical oscillations, he was convinced that matter existed in a state of vibration, but he saw this in terms of a simple physical relationship between objects rather than in the sophisticated concepts of quantum mechanics.

Planet in resonance

In his experiments at Colorado Springs, Tesla had set up a kind of pumping action of electrons in and out of the earth, which he understood as setting up planetary electric currents in resonant motion. It is certainly possible that Tesla's extremely long-wave transmissions could have set up such a resonance. Whether a way can be found to exploit this in the generation of usable energy remains to be seen.

At the other end of the wavelength scale, there is evidence to suggest that Tesla also discovered the principle of the laser. The name 'laser' is an acronym for 'light amplification by stimulated emission of radiation', and the light from a laser is produced by exactly the kind of tuned oscillation that Tesla used to produce his high-voltage discharges, but, of course, at high frequency

John Pierpoint Morgan was head of the most powerful finance house in the United States when he became favourably impressed with the achievements and character of Tesla. His support enabled Tesla to begin work on his 'World System' but, surprisingly, Morgan did not demand a share in the future profits of the enterprise

and short wavelength. It was not until 1960 that the first successful laser was made, when the American physicist T.H. Maiman forced a bar of synthetic ruby to produce red light by 'pumping' light energy into it at exactly the right frequency.

The most important aspect of the light produced by the laser is that it is of a single wavelength. Ordinary light sources produce light of a wide range of wavelengths, which emerges in all directions. Lasers produce light all of one wavelength, the emission moving only in one direction, and with the waves exactly in step (this is called 'coherence'). As a result, a laser beam can be sent over enormous distances without losing its power or being diffused in any way. The first men on the Moon left behind them a reflector designed to send back laser beams transmitted from the Earth. The beams returned without any marked diminution in their power.

Writing in 1934, Tesla described an apparatus that sounds strangely similar to the laser. He claimed it 'projects particles which may be relatively large or of microscopic dimensions, enabling us to convey to a small area at a great distance trillions of times more energy than is possible with rays of any kind. Many thousands of horsepower can thus be transmitted by a stream thinner than a hair, so that nothing can resist.' At his 82nd birthday dinner at the New Yorker hotel in 1938, he was asked 'could he produce an effect on the moon sufficiently large to be seen by an astronomer watching the moon through a high-power telescope?' He replied that he 'would be able to produce in the dark

An electrifying idea

The 'World System' envisioned by Tesla would, according to him, have made possible 'not only the instantaneous and precise wireless transmission of any kind of signals, messages or characters, to all parts of the world, but also the interconnection of the existing telegraph, telephone, and other signal stations without any change in their present equipment.' The radio signals would have been 'non-interfering as well as non-interferable. . . . There is virtually no limit to the number of stations or instruments that can be simultaneously operated without the slightest mutual disturbance.' Tesla described numerous applications. They included the worldwide distribution of news by radio telegraph or radio telephone, and the interconnection of the world's stock market tickertape machines. Clocks of cheap, simple construction would be synchronised anywhere in the world by the system without requiring attention. ('The idea of impressing upon the earth American time is fascinating,' said Tesla, 'and very likely to become popular.') Facsimile transmission of documents would have been possible. A 'universal marine service' would enable ships to steer without compasses. Tesla promised that 'when the first plant is inaugurated . . . humanity will be like an ant heap stirred up with a stick. . . .' The varied means of communication that he foresaw all exist today, and are becoming more widely integrated – but on a principle quite different from Tesla's: by relay from satellites in orbit.

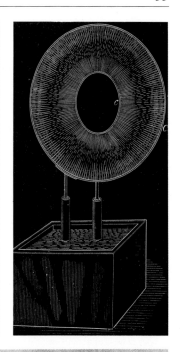

region of the thin crescent new moon an incandescent spot that would glow like a bright star so that it could be seen without the aid of a telescope'.

All this talk on the part of Tesla led to persistent rumours that he had invented a 'death ray', but in an article written in 1935 he stated categorically that 'this invention of mine does not contemplate the use of any so-called "death rays".' He hated war, and he wrote:

We cannot abolish war by outlawing it. We cannot end it by disarming the strong. War can be stopped, not by making the strong weak but by making every nation, weak or strong, able to defend itself. . . . I was fortunate enough to evolve a new idea and to perfect means which can be used chiefly for defense. If it is adopted, it will revolutionize the relations between nations. It will make any country, large or small, impregnable against armies, airplanes, and other means for attack. My invention requires a large plant, but once established it will be possible to destroy anything, men or machines, approaching within a radius of 200 miles [320 kilometres].

Soviet death ray?

In the light of this claim, the concern felt by Major-General George Keegan over the freak electrical storms that occurred over Canada in 1977 takes on a new significance. Major-General Keegan believed that the storms were caused by trials of a Soviet 'particle gun' capable of detonating intercontinental ballistic missiles while still in flight in the upper atmosphere.

The first hints that particle gun experiments were taking place came when satellite data indicated the unexpected presence of hydrogen, with traces of tritium ('heavy

Top: Tesla experimented with various forms of lighting that could be used for advertising. This is a discharge between concentric loops of wire, forming a brilliantly luminous disc that could be used in a display

Above: luminous discharges from the ends of a high-voltage coil. Tesla believed they resembled flames in more than appearance: when fire was fully understood, he thought, it would prove to involve high-frequency electrical fields

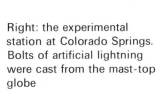
Right: the experimental station at Colorado Springs. Bolts of artificial lightning were cast from the mast-top globe

hydrogen', the fuel of the hydrogen bomb) in the upper atmosphere. Intelligence assessors linked this observation with the information that the Soviets were carrying out experiments at an establishment in Semipalatinsk, Kazakhstan – experiments apparently devoted to the development of a weapon that would accelerate and focus a beam of subatomic particles on a target, such as a missile.

Subatomic particles that could be used in such a weapon are electrons or protons. In modern physical theory, these can be regarded alternatively as tiny solid bodies that can be accelerated by means of the controlled oscillation of an electromagnetic field, or as 'packets' of wave energy that can be 'pumped' forward in exactly the same way as the power is built up by a Tesla coil, or light waves are generated in an intense beam in a laser.

What is particularly significant about a particle gun, or a laser, is that its beam consists of packets of wave energy produced

Below: the all-wooden structure on Long Island that was to be the heart of the World System; it stood until the First World War

at exactly their own inherent frequency, giving what is called a 'coherent' emission – effectively a standing wave of exactly the same kind as that described by Tesla in his paper of 1900.

At an installation code-named 'Tora', at Sary-Shagan, about 500 miles (800 kilometres) from Semipalatinsk, the Soviets have been experimenting with a particle beam weapon since November 1979, and it seems probable that at Gomel, near Minsk, they have been carrying out development work over a considerably longer period. Indeed, what the Soviets vaguely described as 'certain experiments in the high frequency band' caused severe radio blackouts during 1976, leading to protests from several governments, including four from Britain.

Assault on the ionosphere

Of greater importance than such a radio blackout is the possible effect of uncontrolled or – more sinisterly – of controlled firing of a particle beam gun upon the upper atmosphere. At a height of about 65 miles (100 kilometres) above the Earth's surface, the ionosphere begins; this is a series of layers of extremely rarefied air in which atoms are partly broken down into electrically charged ions. The ionosphere is responsible for the reflection of long-wave radio round the globe; it is also the part of the atmosphere in which the remarkable electrical displays of the *aurora borealis* take place, in response to bombardment by cosmic rays from space.

Like a laser, a finely focused particle beam can (almost literally) 'punch' a hole in the ionosphere. The particles – either positively-charged protons or negatively-charged electrons – can seriously affect the distribution of ions around the path of the beam, producing auroral displays and radio blackouts very similar to those recorded over northern Canada in 1977. And who knows what effect these disturbances could have upon currents in the upper atmosphere, and thus upon our weather?

Andrew Michrowski, a scientist working on a power scheme in eastern Canada, had no doubts. 'It is quite clear to me that the Russians are doing experiments based on Tesla's ideas, and in doing so have changed the world's weather,' he said.

Watson W. Scott, director of operations at the Canadian Department of Communications in Ottawa, was even more uncompromising. 'Are these experiments connected with the great [1976] drought in Britain, warm weather in Greenland, snow in Miami? . . . [It] seems to suggest an important new level of competence has been reached in the handling of very powerful physical forces. One person has told me it may be a pinpointing, at last, of the exact frequencies used by Tesla in his work. Those who talk do not necessarily know. Those who know are the sort of people who are paid very good money to say nothing.'

Experience, so most of us believe, leaves its mark on us as a memory stored inside the brain. But is this really the case? RUPERT SHELDRAKE **analyses the evidence – and comes up with a startling new theory**

WE ARE ALL BROUGHT UP to believe that memories are stored inside the brain. It is an old and respectable idea, and many of us may not even think of questioning it. Nevertheless, it may be open to doubt.

The idea that memories are stored inside the brain is known as the trace theory of memory. One of its earliest versions was put forward by Aristotle. He compared memory to impressions left on soft wax by experience: the sealing wax and the impressions left upon it, and the persistence of these impressions in the wax, provided an analogy of the process of memory.

Since Aristotle, this same trace theory has been repeatedly modified in accordance with the latest advances in technology to provide more and more up-to-date analogies. Currently most popular is the theory that memory is stored in the brain in the same way as is the information contained in a hologram (laser photo). This is a sophisticated version of the trace theory, but nevertheless it is essentially the same theory.

The trace theory applies to long-term memory – memories that last over a long period. There is another kind of memory,

How does memory work? Study of the human brain (below) has so far failed to reveal the answer, although many theories have been put forward. One of the most widely accepted is that memories are laid down in the brain in the same way as music is 'stored' in the grooves of a gramophone record (right). Much experimental work has been done in an attempt to locate these 'memory traces', or 'engrams'; so far, however, they have been unsuccessful

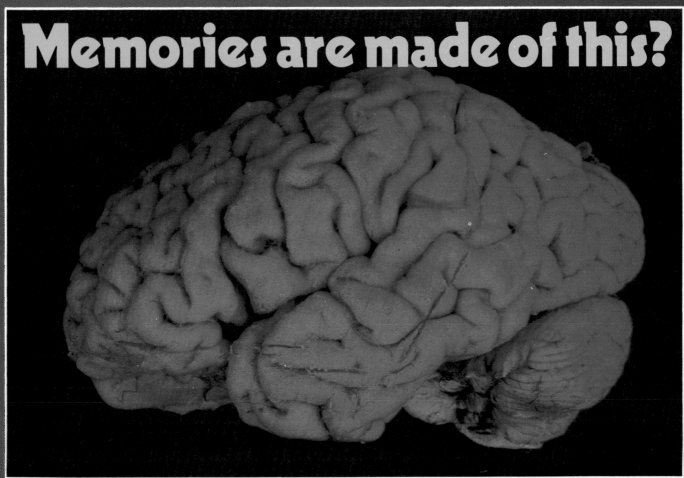

Memories are made of this?

short-term memory – the kind of memory you have when you look up a number in the telephone directory. You remember the number for as long as it takes you to dial it, and then immediately forget it. It is possible that short-term memory is explicable in terms of a kind of reverberation in the brain's neural circuits. It is long-term memory that presents us with problems.

The hypothesis of formative causation suggests one possible answer.

According to this theory, the development of form in living creatures is governed by a morphogenetic field – a kind of biological field that can, by a process called morphic resonance, be 'tuned in' to by *other* members of the same species and so influence their development. This hypothesis can explain memory. If organisms enter into morphic resonance with previous organisms of the same species on the basis of similarity, then there is a very interesting consequence, for the thing that an organism resembles most

provide conclusive and overwhelming evidence for the existence of memory traces, and that lead to the unquestioning acceptance of the idea that memories are stored inside the brain.

The more important of these is the evidence from brain damage – that various types of brain damage can lead to loss of memory. A standard interpretation of this is that the damage has removed those parts of the brain tissue that contain the memory traces. But this is not the only possible interpretation. To see the fallacy in the argument, take the analogy of a television set. If you were to damage a television set by cutting out part of the wiring or removing a few transistors and condensers, and completely lost reception of one channel as a result, you would not automatically assume that this proved that all the people – actors, musicians, announcers – you saw on the programmes of that channel were contained within the condensers and transistors that you had removed. And yet, if

As a result of hydrocephalus – water on the brain – Sharon Scruton (right) has a huge cavity at the centre of her brain; yet she has had a successful school career. Using a technique known as positron emission tomograph – PET – scanning, it is now possible to identify areas of brain activity; these scans (below) show the brain in 'rest state' (left) and exposed to language and music (right). A PET scan of Sharon Scruton's brain reveals that activities that normally take place at the centre of the brain now occur at the peripheries – indicating that specific brain activities are not necessarily linked to specific areas of the brain

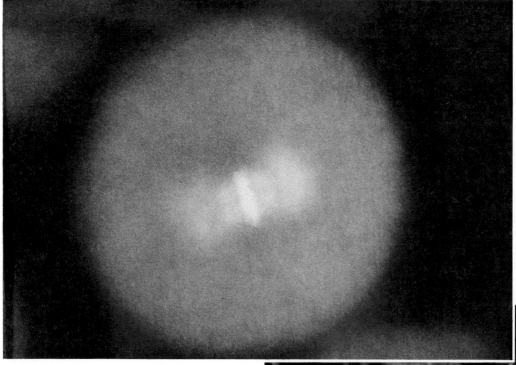

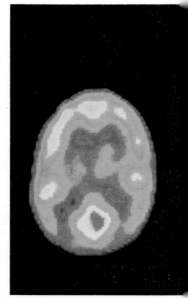

closely in the past is itself. Although it is obvious that the development of individual living things is not governed simply by their own forms in the past, we nevertheless have the fascinating possibility that organisms may be subject to morphic resonance from their own past states.

Memory may consist of a kind of tuning in to the past states of our own organism through the process of morphic resonance – so that the past is, as it were, continuously present to us. Thus, according to this theory, it is not necessary to suppose that memory traces are stored inside the brain.

Why do we take the trace theory of memory for granted? There are two pieces of evidence that, for many people, seem to

electrical stimulation seemed to be reawakening memories. The most obvious interpretation of this result is that the memories must be embedded in the tissue that is stimulated, or near it, and that the electric current somehow reawakens them. This is very often taken as evidence for the trace theory. But again, it is quite inconclusive. Think of the television analogy. If you were to apply electric currents to the tuning circuits inside a television set, you would find some very strange things happening – jumps from channel to channel, possibly, and distortions of the picture. But this does not prove that the figures you see on the television screen are actually located inside the television, any more than in the previous analogy.

Further objections spring from the nature of the trace theory itself. First, it is extremely vague – although the traces are taken for granted, their nature is still very much a matter of dispute in the scientific community. One popular and well-established theory suggests that memories may depend on reverberating circuits of electrical activity in the brain – loops of electrical current within the brain tissue.

Another theory, which was much in vogue during the early 1970s, is the idea that memory is stored in the complex molecules of ribonucleic acid (RNA), a substance that is similar in construction to DNA. The memory traces are, according to this theory, in some unspecified way laid down inside these molecules. This theory has rather gone out of fashion because there is very little evidence to support it, and it is not yet clear how a chemical inside the brain, or a set of chemicals, can fulfil as complex a function as the encoding of memory.

Making connections

The third and most popular of theories of memory is that of synaptic modification. The synapses are the connections between the nerve cells, and the idea is that they somehow become modified as electric pulses – nerve signals – pass through them, making it more likely that the same signals will pass through them again. This is similar to the hydraulic theory of memory proposed by the philosopher and scientist René Descartes (1596-1650). Descartes suggested that memory depended on the flow of fluids through pores. The more often the fluid flowed, the more it would enlarge the pores, making it easy for the fluid to flow in that direction again.

The main evidence for the theory of synaptic modification comes from a series of experiments carried out on a species of snail, *Aplysia*. This snail has exceptionally large nerves, which are therefore easy to study, and it reacts in simple ways to simple stimuli: if you go on prodding it with a needle, for example, it gets used to it after a while and, instead of withdrawing into its shell, it simply ignores it – if, that is, it has established that the stimulus is harmless. This

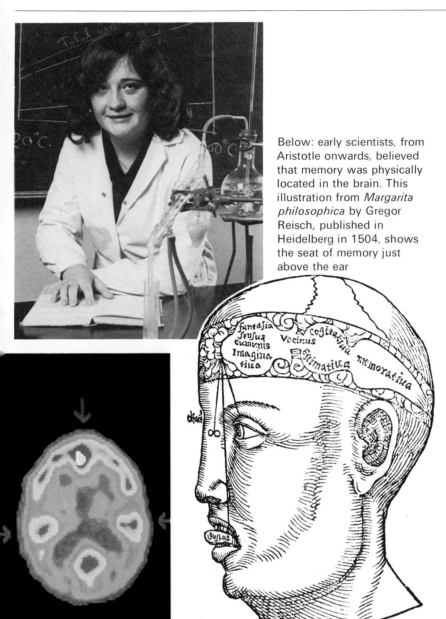

Below: early scientists, from Aristotle onwards, believed that memory was physically located in the brain. This illustration from *Margarita philosophica* by Gregor Reisch, published in Heidelberg in 1504, shows the seat of memory just above the ear

Above left: cells dividing in a sea-urchin's egg, and (left) a fully grown sea-urchin. The development of living creatures, so the accepted theory goes, is governed by a complex chemical, deoxyribonucleic acid – DNA – that is present in every cell. But how does this explain the different ways in which different cells develop – into forms as varied as the sea-urchin's spikes and its luminous blue 'eyes'? A new hypothesis suggests, instead, that living creatures receive their form by 'tuning in' to a 'morphogenetic field' that contains information about the past members of their species

you were embedded in that way of thinking, you might easily think so. And you might think you had proved you were right when you saw that, when you replaced the parts you had removed, the channel reappeared. Loss of memory through brain damage does not prove in any way that memory is stored inside the brain. It merely proves that a normal brain is essential for the effective recall of these memories. It is possible that the effects of brain damage on memory can be explained in terms of the loss of the ability to recall or tune in to past states of the brain. Thus the evidence from brain damage on memory is ambiguous.

A second piece of evidence often cited in favour of the trace theory of memory is the well-known work of Wilder Penfield on the electrical stimulation of the brain tissue of epileptic patients. He found that this enabled some patients to recall particular scenes from their past life with great vividness – the is a well-known kind of learning known as habituation, whereby animals simply ignore stimuli that do not threaten them.

Some very detailed and very elegant experimental work has shown that changes occur in the synapses of *Aplysia* during the process of habituation – but the reason for these changes is still unclear. There is no reason to think that the same kind of change can possibly account for the many and complex kinds of learning that take place in the higher organisms. The evidence shows there certainly are, in some cases, changes in the brain during learning – but can these changes *explain* the phenomenon of memory?

The most damning piece of evidence against the trace theory of memory comes from a series of experiments carried out by K.S. Lashley. He set out with the hypothesis that if memory traces did indeed exist in the brain, it should be possible to locate them. The idea was to cut out portions of the brain and identify the bits of memory that disappeared. He spent a great deal of time doing this and after many years ended up completely frustrated with this line of research. In this passage from an article entitled 'In search of the engram' – engram meaning memory trace – Lashley summarised the work as follows:

> It is not possible to demonstrate the isolated localization of the memory trace anywhere within the nervous system. Limited regions may be essential for learning or retention of a particular activity, but within such regions the parts are functionally equivalent.

Lashley's experiments were on rats, and he found that loss of memory occurred only when large portions of the brain were removed. The loss of memory was proportional to the *amount* of nervous tissue removed, rather than its location. Lashley called this the law of mass action – the idea that it was the mass of tissue removed that was important, not the specific bits. The experiment was repeated with octopuses and the same results were reached – you could cut out bits of the octopus brain, and the loss of memory was proportional to the mass removed, rather than which portion of the brain it was taken from.

The brain as hologram?

Clearly, all attempts to find localised traces within the brain have failed. This, of course, has posed great difficulties for the trace theory of memory, which had earlier seemed quite straightforward. This is the main reason why the holographic theory of memory was developed – a modification that suggested that there are, indeed, memory traces, but they are spread all over the brain so that if you cut parts of it out you won't make much difference, since all the memories are localised everywhere. This theory, clear though it seems, is obscurantist – for, in preserving the idea that memories are located inside the brain, the hypothesis has become almost impossible to test. The brain, after all, is not a hologram. The hologram works on the principle of laser light waves and interference patterns stored on photographic film. There is nothing of the sort in the set-up of the brain.

This is the present state of research into memory. The idea that memory traces are stored inside the brain is really an aspect of the mechanistic theory of life. It all stems from the theory that everything to do with the mind is explicable in terms of matter, and is reducible to things inside the brain. If you share this conviction, then you *have* to believe that memories are inside the brain.

However, when you consider the possibility that the brain may not be a memory

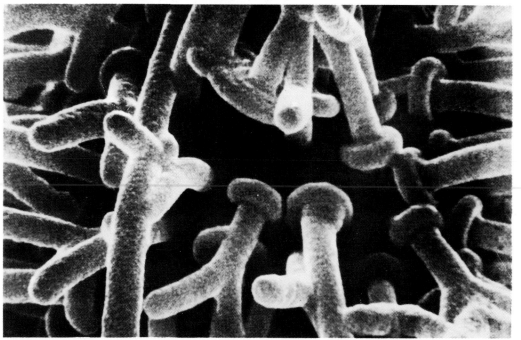

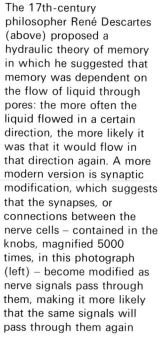

The 17th-century philosopher René Descartes (above) proposed a hydraulic theory of memory in which he suggested that memory was dependent on the flow of liquid through pores: the more often the liquid flowed in a certain direction, the more likely it was that it would flow in that direction again. A more modern version is synaptic modification, which suggests that the synapses, or connections between the nerve cells – contained in the knobs, magnified 5000 times, in this photograph (left) – become modified as nerve signals pass through them, making it more likely that the same signals will pass through them again

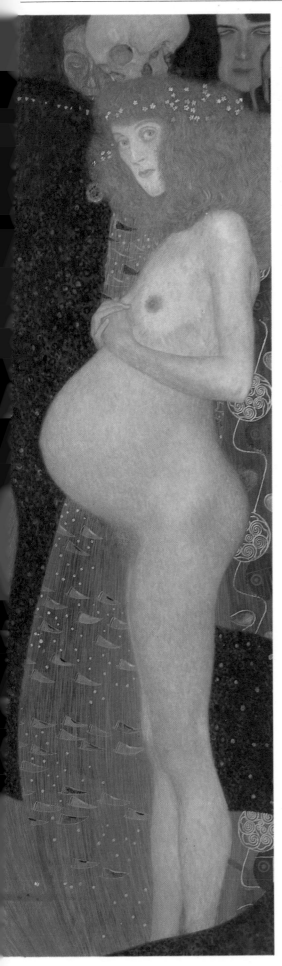

Above: the marine snail *Aplysia punctata*. The main evidence for the theory of synaptic modification comes from study of this snail, which shows changes in its synapses after undergoing a simple learning process

Left: *Hope I*, by Gustav Klimt (1862–1918): a pregnant woman stands surrounded by disturbing and phantasmagorical shapes. Could it be that, through our morphogenetic fields, our thoughts and actions influence human beings, as yet unborn, whom we shall never meet?

storage device, but rather a tuning system that enables memories to be picked up, this failure to find localised memory traces in the brain makes sense. And, startlingly, several hitherto unexplained phenomena may begin to seem less surprising from a scientific point of view.

According to the new theory, we normally 'tune in' to our own memories – but it is conceivable that the process of morphic resonance may allow us to tune in to *other people's*. Telepathy can be explained as the almost instantaneous transfer of very recent memories; clairvoyance could be the result of tuning into the memories of distant people. And there is also, of course, the possibility of tuning in to memories from the distant past. This could be one way of explaining the evidence that people can have access to memories of past lives, often through the process of hypnotic regression. It could even explain why many of the 'memories' produced under hypnotic regression are patchy, or seem to be the result of the overlapping of memories of entirely distinct lives. This could perhaps be the result of tuning in to more than one morphogenetic field at the same time, and jumbling the information received in this way.

The new concept of memory as an aspect of morphic resonance also lends theoretical support to the well-known notion of the collective unconscious put forward by the famous psychologist Carl Gustav Jung. We may be influenced not only by memories of particular people in the past, but also by a sort of pooled or collective memory from countless previous human beings – a sort of species memory. Rather than existing separately, our minds may be influenced directly by other people, including countless people in the past, through the interconnectedness of memory – whether we realise it or not. In turn, our own thoughts and memories may be adding to the collective memory of mankind, and persist to influence future members of the human race.

Is the Earth hollow?

It has long been held that the Earth is hollow – but it was not until 1968 that any proof was forthcoming. In that year, photographs taken by satellite clearly showed an enormous hole at the North Pole. Or did they? W. A. HARBINSON charts the history of this remarkable theory

IN EARLY 1970 the Environmental Science Service Administration of the US Department of Commerce released to the press photographs of the North Pole that had been taken by the ESSA-7 satellite on 23 November 1968. One of the photographs showed the North Pole wreathed in its customary cloud cover; the other, showing the same area without cloud cover, revealed an enormous black hole where the Pole should have been.

Little did the Environmental Science Service Administration know that their routine weather reconnaissance photographs would lead to one of the most sensational and highly publicised controversies in UFO history.

In the June 1970 issue of *Flying Saucers* magazine, editor and ufologist Ray Palmer reproduced the ESSA-7 satellite photographs with an accompanying article that claimed that the enormous hole shown on one of the photographs was real.

It had long been the belief of Ray Palmer and a great many other ufologists that the Earth is hollow, and that the UFOs emerge from and return to a civilisation of superior beings that is hidden in the Earth's unexplored interior. Now, with an actual photograph of an enormous black hole at the North Pole, Palmer was able to assert that his subterranean super race probably existed and could most likely be reached through the holes at the North and South Poles.

According to Palmer, the ESSA-7 satellite

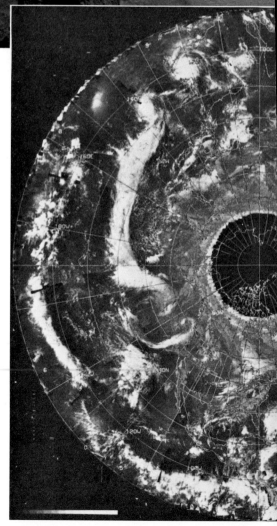

Above: inside a mysterious ice cave at Signy Island, Antarctica

Right: the controversial photograph of the North Pole taken in 1968 by the ESSA-7 satellite, showing a strange black hole where the Pole should be. For certain UFO enthusiasts, this was the ultimate proof that the Earth is hollow

Above: Rear-Admiral Richard
E. Byrd of the US Navy,
whose Polar expeditions
provided inspiration for
believers in the hollow Earth

Below right: Orpheus, whose
wife was kept prisoner in an
underground hell

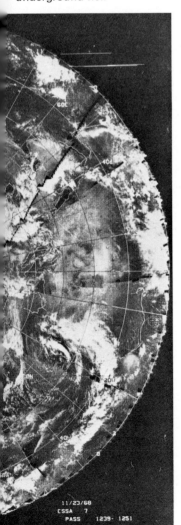

11/23/68
ESSA 7
PASS 1239-1251

photographs were proof that an enormous
hole existed at least at the North Pole, and in
subsequent issues of *Flying Saucers* he
strengthened his case by resurrecting
another long-standing 'hollow Earth' controversy: the famous expeditions of Rear-
Admiral Richard E. Byrd to the North and
South Poles.

Rear-Admiral Richard E. Byrd (1888–
1957) of the US Navy was a distinguished
pioneer aviator and polar explorer who flew
over the North Pole on 9 May 1926 and then
led numerous exploratory expeditions to the
Antarctic, including a flight over the South
Pole on 29 November 1929 and, from 1946 to
1947, his full-scale Operation High Jump,
which was reported to have discovered and
mapped 537,000 square miles (1,390,000
square kilometres) of Antarctic territory.

The land beyond the Pole
Byrd's most famous polar expeditions were
first drawn into the hollow Earth controversy
when a great many articles and books –
notably *Worlds beyond the Poles* (1959) by
Amadeo Giannini and *The hollow Earth*
(1969) by Dr Raymond Bernard – claimed
that Byrd had actually flown, not *across* the
North and South Poles, but *down* into the
great hollows that led into the Earth's
interior. Ray Palmer, quoting extensively
from Giannini's book (as, subsequently, did
Dr Bernard), introduced this theory in the
December 1959 issue of *Flying Saucers* and
thereafter ran a voluminous correspondence
on the subject.

According to Giannini, Bernard and
Palmer, Rear-Admiral Byrd announced in
February 1947, prior to a supposed flight of
1700 miles (2750 kilometres) beyond the
North Pole: 'I'd like to see that *land beyond
the Pole.* That area beyond the Pole is the
centre of the *Great Unknown.*' Giannini,
Bernard and Palmer also claimed that, during
his supposed flight over the North Pole in
February 1947, Rear-Admiral Byrd reported
by radio that he saw below him, not ice and

snow, but land areas consisting of mountains, forests, green vegetation, lakes and
rivers and, in the undergrowth, a strange
animal that resembled a mammoth. Also,
according to Giannini, Bernard and Palmer,
in January 1956, after leading another expedition to the Antarctic, Rear-Admiral
Byrd claimed that his expedition had there
penetrated to a land extent of 2300 miles
(3700 kilometres) *beyond* the South Pole;
and, further, that just before his death in
1957, Rear-Admiral Byrd had called the land
beyond the Pole 'that enchanted continent in
the sky, land of everlasting mystery'. That
land, according to other hollow Earth theorists, was actually the legendary Rainbow
City, home of a fabulous lost civilisation.

For Giannini, Bernard and Palmer, Rear-
Admiral Byrd's reported comments merely
confirmed what they had suspected all along:
that the Earth is shaped 'strangely' at both
Poles, something like a doughnut, with a
depression that either goes down an enormous distance into the bowels of the Earth or
forms a giant hole that actually runs right
through the Earth's core, from one Pole to
the other. Since, geographically speaking, it
would be impossible to fly 1700 miles (2750
kilometres) beyond the North Pole or 2300
miles (3700 kilometres) beyond the South
Pole without seeing water, it then stands to
reason that Rear-Admiral Byrd must have
flown *down* into the enormous convex de-
pressions at the Poles, into the Great
Unknown of the Earth's interior, and that,
had he flown further, he would have arrived
eventually at the secret base of the UFOs
belonging to the hidden super race – perhaps
the legendary Rainbow City that Byrd had
possibly seen reflected in the Antarctic sky.

Thus, when in June 1970 Ray Palmer was
able to publish satellite photographs that
actually showed an enormous black hole at
the North Pole, hollow Earth theorists all
over the world were confirmed in their

beliefs – and the controversy started. But is the Earth really hollow? And do the holes in the Poles exist?

The possibility that the Earth might be hollow, that it may be entered through holes at the North and South Poles, and that secret civilisations still flourish inside it, is one that has fired the imagination since time immemorial. Thus, the Babylonian hero, Gilgamesh, visited an ancestor, Utnapishtim, in the bowels of the Earth; the Greek, Orpheus, tried to rescue his dead wife Eurydice from an underground hell; the Pharaohs of Egypt were rumoured to be in touch with the underworld, which they could reach via secret tunnels concealed in the pyramids; the Incas, in flight from the rapacious Spaniards, reportedly carried much of their treasure into the 'inner Earth'; and the Buddhists believed (and still do) that millions live in Agharta, an underground paradise ruled by the king of the world.

Some illustrious believers

The scientific world was not immune to this theory: Leonard Euler, an 18th-century mathematical genius, deduced that the Earth was hollow, contained a central Sun and was inhabited; and Dr Edmund Halley, discoverer of Halley's comet and Astronomer Royal for England in the 18th century, also thought that the Earth was hollow and contained inside it three planets. In the early 1870s, John Cleves Symmes, a Civil War hero, almost obtained United States government backing for an expedition to prove his theories that the Earth was hollow, and in 1878 his son published Symmes's theories in a book, *The Symmes theory of concentric spheres, demonstrating that the Earth is hollow, habitable within and widely open about the Poles*, thereby hoping to persuade the world that the interior of the Earth could be reached through large holes at the North and South Poles, and that inside the Earth would be found 'a warm and rich land, stocked with thrifty vegetables and animals, if not men'. Among those who jumped onto the Symmes's bandwagon were Cyrus Read Teed, who founded a hollow Earth religion; William Reed, who wrote the controversial book, *Phantom of the Poles* (1906); and, of course, Symmes's son, who added to his father's fanciful theory the even more fanciful notion that the inhabitants of the inner Earth were the 10 lost tribes of Israel.

None of these theories was supported by anything other than wishful thinking, but they sat comfortably side by side with various works of fiction on the subject, the most notable of which were Edgar Allan Poe's *Narrative of Arthur Gordon Pym* (1833), in which the hero and his companion have a chilling confrontation with emissaries from the interior; and Jules Verne's *Journey to the centre of the Earth* (1864), in which an adventurous professor, his nephew and a guide enter the inner Earth through an

The Earth turned inside out

If *Journey to the centre of the Earth* remains the most popular of the hollow Earth novels, perhaps the one with the most baleful influence was Edward Bulwer-Lytton's *The coming race* (1871), in which the hero descends into a deep mine and finds himself in a subterranean world inhabited by highly advanced, vindictive beings who have harnessed 'Vril fluid', a kind of energy that can be conducted over vast distances and used

A leaflet entitled *The Earth – with a new map of our enclosed world* by the Dowager Lady Blount, published in 1921. Her view of the Earth's 'real' structure was similar to that of certain Nazis; the Earth is concave and 'the heavens' are inside the cavity of the southern hemisphere

extinct volcano in Iceland, and there encounter new skies, seas and giant, prehistoric reptiles roaming the forests.

Nonetheless, the belief in a hollow Earth was so widespread that even Edgar Rice Burroughs felt obliged to write *Tarzan at the Earth's core* (1929), in which the famous child of the jungle goes to Pellucidar, a world lying on the inner surface of the Earth and lit by a central Sun. If this creation had a lot in common with the fiction of Bulwer-Lytton and the perverted romanticism of the Vril Society, H. P. Lovecraft's *The shadow out of time* (1936) brought the theme into the modern age by introducing an ancient, subterranean race that had dominated the Earth 150 million years ago and has since, in the safety of the inner Earth, invented airships and atomic-powered vehicles, and mastered time-travel and ESP.

There can be little doubt that Lovecraft's famous novel influenced the much-discussed *I remember Lemuria* by Richard S. Shaver, a lengthy article first published in the March 1945 issue of *Amazing Stories* magazine and claimed, by the author, to be fact rather than mere fiction. In his article, Shaver stated that the interior of the Earth is laced with a network of gigantic caves, that the caves are filled with a race of malformed, subhuman for good or evil. Vril fluid in some ways resembles the power of Kundalini, the spinal fire of Tantric tradition. The inhabitants of this subterranean world, Vril-ya, descended into the Earth during the Flood, but are planning to return to the surface world to conquer an intellectually decadent mankind.

Bulwer-Lytton's novel proved the inspiration of various occult groups, including the 'Luminous Lodge' or Vril Society, which was established in the early days of Nazi Germany. The members of the Vril Society confused Bulwer-Lytton's fiction with their own murky visions of an Aryan master race inhabiting the lost world of Thule which, according to legend, disappeared 'somewhere in the far north'. They were determined that, when this master race returned to the Earth's surface, they would be their equals and not slaves.

Loosely connected with these beliefs was the persistent theory that the Earth possessed concave curvature, so that mankind lived *inside* the globe, with a small Sun and tiny starry heaven at its centre. So insistent on this theory were certain members of the Nazi Party that in April 1942 Dr Heinz Fisher and a group of leading scientists were sent to the Baltic island of Rugen with a mass of radar equipment to obtain reflections of radar beams from the far side of the Earth. They returned in defeat.

advanced beings inhabiting the interior of the Earth. The flying saucers left and re-entered this world via enormous holes at the North and South Poles.

Such theories led to a resurrection of belief in the 'lost' civilisations of Atlantis, Lemuria and Thule, with the latter, in particular, now thought to be located in the Arctic. (Not to be confused with Dundas, formerly Thule, the Eskimo settlement in north-west Greenland that is now a major US air base and communications centre.) However, it was also widely believed that another likely source of the UFOs was to be found in the Antarctic. This theory was encouraged by the publication of John G. Fuller's remarkably persuasive factual book, *The interrupted journey* (1966), in which the author tells the story of Betty and Barney Hill, an American couple who, during psychiatric treatment for an inexplicable period of amnesia, recalled under hypnosis that they had been temporarily abducted by extra-terrestrials, examined inside a flying saucer, and informed that the extra-terrestrials had secret bases located all over the Earth, some of them under the sea, and at least one in the Antarctic.

This sensational case, coupled with Aimé Michel's widely read *Flying saucers and the straight-line mystery* (1958) – from which many people deduced that the saucers generally flew in north-southerly directions – strengthened the growing belief in the Arctic and Antarctic as the likely locations of the secret bases of the flying saucers.

So it happened that when in June 1970

creatures called *deros* or *abandonderos* (so called because they abandoned the surface Earth 12,000 years ago), that the *deros* had once been slaves of a Lemurian master race that now existed in outer space, and that they now occupied themselves by persecuting the humans of the surface world and were therefore responsible for some of the world's most momentous calamities.

Shaver's insistence that a Lemurian underworld actually existed – and that he had been taken down into it by some *deros* – was given enormous publicity in the United States, leading to a resurgence of interest in the possibility of a hollow Earth and hidden, highly advanced civilisations; so it was perhaps not an accident that the UFO age was ushered in two years later, on 21 June 1947, with the reported sighting of five disc-shaped unidentified aircraft over the Canadian border by Harold Dahl and, three days later, by Kenneth Arnold's famous sighting of 'flying saucers' over the Cascade Mountains in the USA.

After those two sightings, UFO mania swept the United States and eventually the world. Two of the most popular theories were that the UFOs were either extra-terrestrial spacecraft from some distant galaxy or belonged to a species of highly

Top: John Cleves Symmes, the 19th-century American hollow Earth theorist who believed the inner world to be 'a warm and rich land, stocked with thrifty vegetables and animals, if not men'

Above: an illustration of 'the central sea' from Jules Verne's *Journey to the centre of the Earth*

Right: Betty and Barney Hill, alleged UFO abductees whose captors explained that there were many UFO bases in or under the Earth – and even under the sea

Far left: the Babylonian hero Gilgamesh who visited an ancestor inside the Earth

Ray Palmer published his controversial theory that flying saucers belonged to a hidden civilisation inside the Earth and emerged from enormous 'holes' at the Poles of the kind shown on the ESSA-7 satellite photographs – and coupled this with his equally sensational revelations about Rear-Admiral Byrd's flights down into the uncharted depths of the concave Antarctic – ufologists and hollow Earth believers all over the world sat up and took notice. Was this the final proof?

Misinterpreted satellite pictures, an explorer's twisted words and an age-old belief – is this all the evidence for the hollow Earth?

The solid facts

JUST HOW MUCH TRUTH was contained in the assertions of Palmer, Bernard and Giannini and the other leading believers in the hollow Earth? Alas, very little.

The most extensive research has offered no confirmation for any of the extraordinary statements attributed to Rear-Admiral Byrd – nor for his reported flight over the North Pole in February 1947. (Byrd flew over the *South* Pole on 16 February 1947, during his extensive Operation High Jump.) Even accepting that Byrd *did* make such comments, it is more reasonable to assume that 'the land beyond the Pole' and the 'Great Unknown' are merely descriptive phrases for hitherto unexplored regions rather than for unknown continents hidden in a hollow Earth – and that the 'enchanted continent in the sky' was merely a description of a common phenomenon in Antarctic conditions – the mirage-like reflection of land.

But what, precisely, did Rear-Admiral Byrd say? In extracts from his journal, published in the *National Geographic* magazine of October 1947, he wrote: 'As I write this, we are circling the South Pole. . . . The Pole is approximately 2500 feet [760 metres] below us. On the other side of the Pole we are looking into that vast unknown area we have struggled so hard to reach.'

Where the mammoth roams

Did Byrd claim to have flown 1700 miles (2750 kilometres) beyond the North Pole in February 1947? No. Describing his flight beyond the *South* Pole on 16 February 1947, he wrote: 'We flew to approximately latitude 88°30' south, an estimated 100 miles [160 kilometres]. Then we made approximately a right-angle turn eastward until we reached the 45th east meridian, when we turned again, this time on our way back to Little America.'

There are even some people who maintain that they saw a newsreel feature on Byrd's flight over the North Pole, showing 'its mountains, trees, river, and a large animal identified as a mammoth'. One woman wrote to Ray Palmer about this alleged newsreel, claiming to have seen it in White Plains, New York, in 1929. She ends her letter:

Byrd narrated this film himself and exclaimed in wonder as he approached a warm water lake surrounded by conifers, with a large animal moving about among the trees, and what Byrd described as a mountain of coal, sparkling with diamonds.

Intriguing though this 'short' would have been, there is no record of it now in any

archive. A US Government cover-up? Or did the film ever really exist in the first place? It is curious how believers 'remember' in good faith a film that was almost certainly never taken – though apparently many of our early memories are 'invented'.

Did Byrd report seeing on that journey, not ice and snow, but land areas consisting of mountains, forests, green vegetation, lakes and rivers and, in the 'undergrowth', a strange animal that resembled a mammoth? No. According to his journal: 'Altogether we had surveyed nearly 10,000 square miles [25,900 square kilometres] of "the country beyond the Pole". As was to be expected, although it is somewhat disappointing to report, there was no observable feature of any significance beyond the Pole. There was only the rolling white desert from horizon to horizon.'

Wishful thinking about such legendary lost worlds as Thule and the Antarctic's Rainbow City inexorably led to even more colourful distortions of fact.

What of the fabled Rainbow City? This is almost certainly an offspring of Rear-Admiral Byrd's original description of his flight back from the South Pole in February 1947, over hitherto unexplored country between the Beardmore and Wade Glaciers. 'It

Above: taken on the Apollo 17 Moon mission, this view of Earth shows Antarctica clearly. Before the technical advances of the 20th century, Man could only guess at the formation of the planet. Now Earth has been photographed from space and analysed with the most sensitive equipment, is it clear how it was formed?

Below: Admiral Byrd – did he discover a hollow Earth?

might have been called the Avenue of Frozen Rainbows,' Byrd wrote. 'To east and west towered great mountains. Some were free of ice – coal black and brick red. Others were completely ice-covered. These looked like titanic waterfalls. Where the sun struck their peaks and slopes the light was reflected from them in an indescribable complex of colours. There were blends of blues, purples, and greens such as man seldom has seen.'

Thus, given Byrd's actual words as distinct from those attributed to him, we can see that neither lush green lands nor living mammoths were seen beyond the South Pole; that the quoted figure of 1700 miles (2750 kilometres) beyond the Pole, even if not invented, was probably extrapolated from an original figure given in square miles; that Rainbow City has no substance other than as Byrd's descriptive 'Avenue of Frozen Rainbows' – a normal atmospheric phenomenon in the Antarctic; and that 'the land beyond the Pole' and/or the 'Great Unknown' were merely, in Byrd's own words, 'the vastest unknown which remains in the world'.

Nonetheless, could the Earth still be hollow? Again, the answer has to be negative. Contrary to the assertions of the hollow Earth theorists, the physical properties and structure of the Earth's interior can now be accurately measured with seismometers and electronic computers. Far from being hollow, the Earth is composed of three principal layers: the crust, the mantle and the core. The crust of granite and basalt rock is up to 25 miles (40 kilometres) thick (much

thinner beneath the deep oceanic basins). Below the crust is the mantle, extending downwards for about 1800 miles (2900 kilometres), solid and composed of magnesium silicates, iron, calcium and aluminium. And below this is the core, believed to be predominantly composed of metallic iron in the molten state. Finally, at a depth of about 3160 miles (5090 kilometres), is the boundary of the inner core, which may be solid as the result of the iron freezing under the extraordinary pressure of about 3,200,000 atmospheres. Certainly, then, the Earth is not remotely hollow.

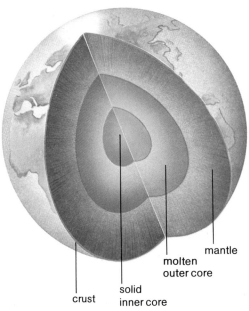

Right: diagram showing the geological composition of the Earth. The planet consists of crust, mantle and core; any hollow part exists only in the imagination

mantle

molten outer core

solid inner core

crust

And what of the enormous hole apparently shown on the satellite photograph of the Arctic regions? The explanation is absurdly simple and could have been thought of by an intelligent child who knew something of the Earth's daily rotation. Unfortunately, the hollow Earth enthusiasts seized on the photograph as 'proof' without reference to such a level of expertise.

The photograph is a mosaic of television images gathered by the satellite over 24 hours, showing the Earth from many angles. The images were processed by a ground computer and reassembled to form a single composite view of the Earth as if viewed from a single point directly over the Pole. During the 24 hours, every point in the middle and equatorial latitudes received sunlight for a period, and so appears on the composite picture. But regions near the Pole were experiencing the continuous darkness of the northern winter. Hence an unlit area occupies the centre of the picture.

Similar pictures made during the northern summer show the polar ice-cap. So do pictures made at any time of year using infrared (heat) wavelengths, since the Earth sends out heat radiation during both day and night.

In short, there are no holes at the Poles – and the Earth is not hollow.

Below: a mosaic, or composite photograph of the North Pole taken from a meteorological satellite during the summer of 1973. Here the polar area is adequately lit but in winter the North Pole is in continuous darkness – and in photographs appears as a large black 'hole'

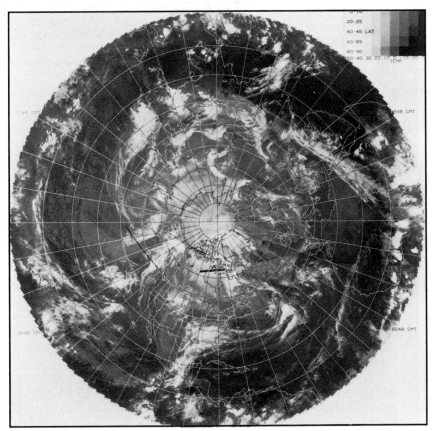

Jesus was crucified in ancient Edinburgh; Bath was classical Athens . . . these were among the colourful views of patriot, journalist and crank Comyns Beaumont. PETER JAMES examines Beaumont's fantastic ideas

INVESTIGATION INTO THE MYSTERIES of the ancient world can be a head-spinning task. Not many authors feel they have hit upon *the* solution to age-old problems of history and religion, and have then pursued their flash of inspiration through thick and thin, disregarding all the evidence to the contrary. Such an approach is definitely the hallmark of a crank, though this is a label to be applied with care. Dr Immanuel Velikovsky, controversial author of *Worlds in collision* was accused of crankery and persecuted on the publication of his astounding and far-reaching claims, which flew in the face of the conventional view of world history.

But Velikovsky was not the first to attempt such a massive revision of the accepted view of world history. A previous, even more extreme, stab at a grand rewriting of the past had been made in the 1940s by the eccentric English theorist Comyns Beaumont. Like Velikovsky a catastrophist, Beaumont developed his own theory of a collision between the Earth and an enormous comet. He also went on, like Velikovsky, to question the accepted dates for various geological ages, and composed his own version of Egyptian history.

But where Velikovsky was satisfied with suggesting a 'revised chronology' for the ancient world, Beaumont went further still and beguiled his readers with the remarkable idea of a 'revised geography' for Man's history. In three volumes, he presented the

Right: the hanging gardens of Babylon – a beautiful, if decadent, centre of ancient civilisation, which archaeologists place in modern Iraq. Comyns Beaumont, however, knew better – it was clearly Rome, a city comparable in splendour and sin

Far right: mosaic in St Mark's, Venice, showing scenes from the story of Noah and the Flood. Beaumont considered Mesopotamia an unlikely spot for the Deluge – the Atlantic, he claimed, was the real site

Britain's greatest crank

Unfettered by considerations of logic or proof, Comyns Beaumont (left) developed a meticulous 'revised geography' to show that all the important classical and biblical sites were in Britain (right) which, many thousands of years ago, had also been Atlantis

case for one of the most fantastic assertions ever to reach the printed page – that all the events described in the Bible, and most of those in Greek myth and history, took place on the soil of the British Isles or closely neighbouring countries. The geography of the ancient world had been distorted, he argued, by the misunderstandings (or deliberate falsifications) of later Greek and Roman historians, and the 'truth' had been covered up. It was Beaumont's privilege to 'rediscover' the ancient centres of Israel, Judah, Greece and Egypt in the green and pleasant lands of England, Scotland and Wales. His theories made the far-fetched claims of the 'British Israelites' – Victorian eccentrics who believed the Anglo-Saxons were descended from the 'lost tribes of Israel' – seem restrained.

Strange though it may seem, there is no good reason to believe that Comyns Beaumont was actually insane. Born into a

family of landed gentry claiming descent from the Normans, he worked for a while in diplomatic service before becoming a journalist. He enjoyed a long and successful, albeit chequered, career as editor and writer for a host of English newspapers and popular magazines, playing an important part in the publishing business throughout the difficult years of two world wars. Yet, although he was extremely intelligent and erudite, Beaumont completely cast loose from the anchor of reason in a ruthless pursuit of his *idée fixe* – that Britain had been the motherland of world civilisation, an idea epitomised in the title of his last book: *Britain: key to world history*.

Although it is difficult to follow much of the reasoning behind Beaumont's extravagant proposals, one can trace out a fascinating, if disjointed, trail of wayward logic in his work, which began with some intriguing speculations but led to confusion and eventually self-contradiction.

In the foreword to *The middle of prehistoric Britain* Beaumont explained how he 'stumbled rather than deliberately walked into a recognition that the history of remote days as passed down was based on false

premises in regard to the most famous of ancient peoples, both in regard to geography and chronology'. He was originally fascinated by the perennial problem of the location of Atlantis, the legendary cradle of civilisation, now apparently submerged beneath the waves. Since the Greek philosopher Plato – to whom we owe the original Atlantis story – located the island in the Atlantic Ocean, Beaumont had little difficulty in following his patriotic inclinations and identifying it with the British Isles. Here, after all, are to be found the earliest traces of human habitation of any of the Atlantic islands. And the story of Atlantis's destruction, he reasoned, concerned the break-up of an extended British land-mass that once stretched towards Scandinavia, resulting in the formation of the islands now known as the Shetlands, Hebrides and Orkneys.

Then came the deluge
In Plato's account, the rich and powerful Atlanteans became corrupted by centuries of materialistic indulgence. Annoyed with their immorality, the gods destroyed their land with earthquake and flood. As Beaumont – and many others – noticed, this motif of a degenerate first race destroyed by natural catastrophe neatly parallels the biblical (and ancient Near Eastern) story of Noah's Flood, sent by God to obliterate the sinful.

Many have argued that a common origin for such myths, even the possibility of a real universal deluge, should be considered. But Beaumont had the temerity to turn the tables completely on the traditional view and insist that the Flood had taken place in Britain rather than Mesopotamia. And if the Flood was an Atlantic event, then maybe Noah, and even the Hebrew patriarchs who followed him, were not really at home in the Near East, but in north-west Europe. Beaumont mused on the antiquity of the human remains from the Atlantic coastal region, from the cave-paintings of the Dordogne to the profusion of megalithic remains found in the Orkneys. The Near East, at least at the time

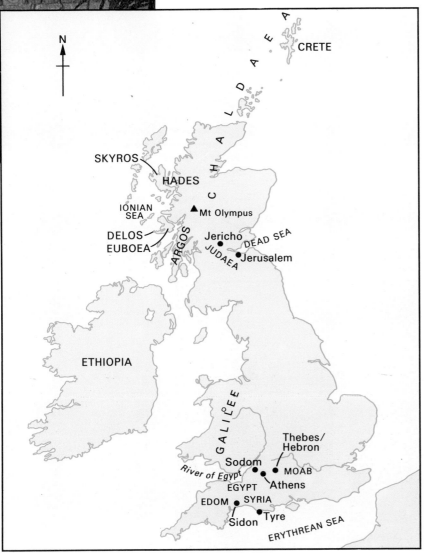

of Beaumont's writing, seemed to have comparatively little to offer in terms of prehistoric remains. For Beaumont it was logical to assume that north-west Europe was the real home of civilisation and the cradle of mankind described in so many mythologies – call it Atlantis, Merope, Crete or the Garden of Eden.

He easily mustered support for this flash of inspiration with a hotch-potch of legends from many Old World cultures telling of a land of the gods, spirits or the dead that lay in the west. The widespread idea of a spirit land to the west is actually almost certainly due to the fact that this is the direction of the setting – or 'dying' – Sun. But Beaumont preferred a literal interpretation. Wringing every geographical clue he could from the myths, he fearlessly identified the Hades of Greek myth (the Amentet of the ancient Egyptians) with a group of islands off the coast of western Scotland. His feverish imagination led him to see, in the innocent Loch Carron and the nearby hamlet of Erbusaig, the hellish river Acheron and the Greek purgatory Erebus. The famous burning river of Hades, the Styx, was seen in Loch Alsh and became the starting point for Beaumont's next extraordinary theoretical leap. The Greek hero Achilles was dipped in the river Styx by his mother to make him immortal, and then spent his childhood on the rocky island of Skyros. With great excitement Beaumont relates the striking confirmation of his theory – at the mouth of Loch Alsh lay the island of Skye, 'unmistakably' Skyros!

After this revelation, there was no turning back. Skyros, unlike Erebus and Acheron, was not a mythical place but a historical location. To make things fit, Beaumont studiously shunted the various countries of classical Greece known to surround Skyros around the Scottish Highlands. He followed this up by scattering the peoples and places of the Old Testament around the map of Britain. Having taken the plunge, Beaumont

Left: Achilles is dipped into the Styx to make him immortal. Beaumont believed that Loch Alsh (below) was the Styx and that Skyros, where Achilles was said to grow up, was the Isle of Skye

Below left: Bath, a city with a long history. But none of its records mentions that it was once commonly known as Athens (below right), as Beaumont claimed. Take away the B and add 'ens' – and Bath becomes Athens, said Beaumont

dived deeper and deeper into the gulf of speculation and came up with what seemed to him to be pearls. Surely, he reasoned, the Ionian Greeks had lived in Iona. The Scottish partiality for the name Alexander clearly reflected the days when Alexander the Great had lorded it over the British Isles. And weren't the Faeroe Islands so called because they were once ruled over by a pharaoh?

Site by site, all the important centres of the ancient world were whisked away from the Mediterranean and Near East and arranged into a fantastic constellation around the North Sea. Wales became Galilee, Somerset Egypt and the river Severn the Nile. Hamburg in Germany, not Hissarlik in Turkey, had been the site of the Trojan War. Babylon was clearly Rome, not some insignificant mud-heap in Iraq. Snowy Ben Nevis was graced with the title of Olympus, home of the Greek gods. And the inhabitants of Bristol – had they known – would have been surprised to learn that their city was really Sodom, renowned in the Bible for its wickedness. The crowning glory of Beaumont's work was to discover the 'real' location of the holy city of Jerusalem, and to

Right: Xerxes leads his army to attack Greece. Beaumont corrected the errors of centuries and relocated Greece in Britain. Xerxes, he said, had to march through Scotland to reach it

Below left: Egyptian hieroglyphics on the wall of a tomb in Egypt – not Scotland, as Beaumont believed. He used the Egyptian Book of the Dead to 'prove' that the Egyptian Underworld was really Fingal's Cave on the Scottish Isle of Staffa (below)

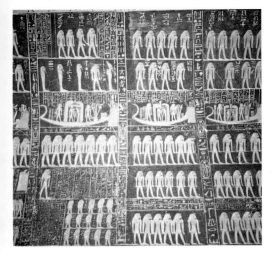

trace the events leading to Christ's crucifixion through the streets of Edinburgh.

By now completely up a gum-tree, Beaumont's enthusiasm had led him into a world of inconsistent and facile methodology. While using the translation of the ancient Egyptian Book of the Dead to 'prove' that Fingal's Cave on the Scottish island of Staffa was the location of the Egyptian Underworld, he also had to deny that Egyptian hieroglyphics had been deciphered – he even asserted they were, in fact, untranslatable gibberish. And when we are asked by him to believe that Athens was really Bath – because one can ignore the B and add 'ens' – then it obviously becomes superfluous to subject Beaumont's work to any serious critique. One should simply enjoy it. Beaumont's work became so undisciplined that any hope of scientific merit was left by the wayside. But he takes the prize for sheer extravagance of imagination.

It is to be regretted that Beaumont's promised further study of ancient history was never published. In this he planned to show how geography had been distorted by the massive migrations of peoples from Britain and by the deliberate falsification of Greek historians such as Herodotus and Thucydides. We were also to be entertained to an account of how Xerxes's Persian army

Below: Thucydides, one of the wayward Greek historians responsible for the widespread prejudice against an English Greece – according to Beaumont. In fact, every single historian was seen as a liar or a cheat. Only Beaumont was right

had marched through Scotland to attack a Greece relocated through the length of the British Isles.

How a man of Beaumont's undoubted intelligence can have so deluded himself is difficult to imagine, but the *why* is clear. Beaumont was motivated by an intense patriotism, a force that coloured his career as an editor and journalist as well as his view of ancient history. Basically liberal, but intensely nationalist, his greatest belief was in Britain as the fount and mainstay of democracy, and he drifted from newspaper to newspaper in an endless quest for a publication that he felt really served the interests of the British people rather than that of financial operators. The ups and downs of his career were described in his autobiography, *A rebel in Fleet Street*.

Were he alive today, Beaumont would have been delighted to learn that ancient Europe's role in the rise of civilisation has now been restored by the archaeological discoveries of the 1970s. But nothing, unfortunately – apart from the acrobatics of an overwrought imagination – can ever transfer the scene of biblical stories and Greek myth to Beaumont's beloved homeland. Egypt remains in Egypt, and Greece remains in Greece, despite the earnest endeavours of Britain's greatest crank.

From simple telepathic commands to world domination through mind control – is this the inevitable progress of Soviet psi? GUY LYON PLAYFAIR begins a disturbing series on psychical research in the USSR

'HUMAN INTELLIGENCE has discovered much in nature that was hidden,' wrote Lenin, 'and it will discover much more, thus strengthening its domination over her.' And although in the aftermath of the 1918 Bolshevik Revolution he did his best to stamp out non-materialist superstitions and beliefs, before Lenin's death in 1924 the young Soviet Union had become the first country in the world to provide official support for research into nature's most baffling area – that which was later to be called parapsychology. Thus an official interest dating back at least to 1891 – when the Russian Society for Experimental Psychology was founded to study psychic phenomena – was maintained unbroken.

Half a century later, it was clear that Soviet scientists had learned a good deal about this 'hidden' branch of knowledge, and were ready to put their discoveries to good use. There is a very sinister ring to some of their terminology, such as 'distant influence', 'mental suggestion' and 'transfer of motor impulses' – in other words, making people act and think according to instructions of which they are not consciously aware. The theme of domination, as forecast by Lenin, runs through much Soviet work in parapsychology, and little imagination is needed to speculate on the uses to which such practices can be, and perhaps *are* being, put.

Soviet interest in psychic matters was not initially inspired by Lenin, nor even by a scientist, but a circus performer named Vladimir Durov, one of the most skilful animal trainers of all time. His animals, especially his dogs, delighted audiences with their well-rehearsed tricks. Although these were produced not by telepathy but by thorough training and the use of signals from an ultrasonic whistle, Durov was convinced that he could make direct mind-to-mind contact with his performers and persuade them to carry out tasks far more complex than their routine circus stunts.

'Suppose,' he said, 'we have

A psychic revolution

The Kremlin in Moscow. Behind these walls Soviet military leaders and politicians are believed to be planning to use psychotronic weapons against the West

Above right: Vladimir Bekhterev, whose pioneering work on animal behaviour led him to experiment with human mind control

the following task: to suggest that the dog go to a table and fetch a book lying upon it. . . . I take his head between my hands, as if I am symbolically inculcating in him the thought that he is entirely in my power. . . . I fix my eyes upon his. . . .' Durov would then visualise the exact nature of the task to be performed, adding: 'I fix into his brain what I just before fixed in my own. I mentally put before him the part of the floor leading to the table, then the leg of the table, then the tablecloth, and finally the book.' Then, on the *mental* command, the dog would rush off 'like an automaton', leap onto the table and seize the book in its teeth.

After watching Durov and his dogs perform at a circus, one of the country's leading scientists, Academician Vladimir Bekhterev (1857–1927), a colleague of reflexologist Ivan Pavlov, decided to put his claims to the test in his laboratory. After several demonstrations, which involved different dogs, Bekhterev

Vladimir Durov, one of the most popular stars of the Moscow circus, with one of his trained wolves (above right) and sealions (right). His discovery of how to convey commands to his dogs through mental suggestion inspired Bekhterev to experiment with telepathy in humans. Durov first took the dog's head in his hands to impress it with his control over it, then visualised, as vividly as possible, the dog doing the task he was about to set. He would then issue a mental command – and the dog would instantly rush off 'like an automaton' and complete the task

was satisfied that animal behaviour could be influenced by 'thought suggestion' even when dog and trainer were out of sight of each other. Some of the tests, carried out in Durov's absence, involved tasks known only to Bekhterev himself, and he even achieved limited success with his own dog.

Inconclusive as it was, Bekhterev's work with Durov encouraged him to take telepathy seriously. On becoming head of the Brain Research Institute at Leningrad University, he founded a Commission for the Study of Mental Suggestion in 1922 and set to work – not with dogs, but with humans as subjects. In one series of experiments, successful attempts were made to 'send' visual images to a subject who was told to write or draw whatever came into her mind. An extract from the sender's notes reads:

Transmitted: triangle with a circle inside it. The subject completes the task [draws the target] at once.

Transmitted: a simple pencil drawing of an engine. The percipient carries out the task precisely, and goes over the contour of the engine several times.

Members of the commission then tried concentrating on objects instead of drawings, and found that while subjects rarely identified the object itself, they often picked up unmistakable features of it, and even the sender's mental associations with it. A subject whose target was a block of cut glass reported 'reflections in water – sugar loaf – snowy summit – iceberg, ice floes in the north illuminated by the sun – rays are broken up'. In another experiment, the sender stared at a framed portrait of a woman and noticed a reflection on its glass surface from a light bulb in the shape of the letter N. 'Napoleon – the letter N flashed by,' he said to his assistant. A minute later, the subject, who was out of earshot, announced, 'I see either Napoleon or Vespasian.' Altogether, the commission ran 269 experiments in transmission of objects or images, and reported that no less than 134 were wholly or partly successful.

At the 1924 Congress of Psychoneurology, delegates were given a spontaneous demonstration of telepathic control in action. On his way to the meeting, Professor K. I. Platonov happened to meet one of his patients, whom he asked to come along without telling her why. Then, in full view of the audience, Platonov put the girl to sleep in a matter of seconds by mental suggestion from behind a blackboard, then woke her by the same method. Afterwards, the girl asked him: 'Why did you invite me to the Congress? I don't understand. What happened to me? I slept, but I don't know why. . . .' Platonov later revealed that this subject was so suggestible that he could send her to sleep even while she was dancing a waltz.

His experiment was repeated independently, and at almost the same time, by a group of researchers at the University of Kharkhov, where psychologist Dr K. D. Kotkov reported that a series of about 30 experiments, held over a two-month period and designed to influence the behaviour of a girl student, were *all* successful. He described exactly how he did it.

He would sit quietly and mentally murmur the words of suggestion to his subject. Then he would visualise her doing what he wished, and finally he would strongly *wish* her to do so. (This last stage was, he felt, the most important.) In this way he could not only send the girl to sleep and wake her up, but even 'summon' her to the laboratory. When asked why she had turned up, the bewildered girl replied, 'I don't know. I just did. I wanted to come.' The

Above: Professor K.I. Platonov, prize-winning Soviet mathematician. He caused a sensation at the 1924 Congress of Psychoneurology by putting a female subject to sleep merely by mentally suggesting (while hidden from her sight) that she do so. When she woke up she had no conscious knowledge of the experiment. Platonov later stated that this girl was so suggestible that she could be mentally commanded to go to sleep even while she was dancing – instantly falling asleep on cue. The implications of this are far reaching, for who knows how many people are similarly ill-equipped to withstand mental manipulation?

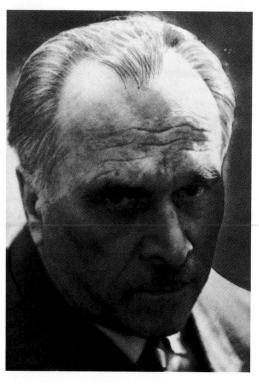

Left: Professor Leonid Vasiliev, a former student of Bekhterev. Vasiliev grew up with a personal experience of telepathy and made it his life's work to study the phenomenon objectively. He proved that it is possible to send someone to sleep even at a distance of 1000 miles (1600 kilometres) away. But he never managed to discover a physical explanation for telepathy

most alarming aspect of this early example of behaviour control was that at no time was the girl aware of what was happening. 'When are the experiments about which you warned me going to start?' she kept asking – even after they had been carried out.

In addition to its own research, Bekhterev's commission studied reports of spontaneous telepathy – which the Revolution had not managed to suppress totally – from members of the public. One well-documented case concerned a student who had seen a bright light on his bedroom wall 'transforming itself into the clear head of a young lady'. He recognised her as his friend Nadezhda. 'After smiling at me,' he reported, 'she spoke a sentence of which I only managed to catch the last word – "decay". Then the girl's image seemed to melt into the wall and disappear.' The student wrote out an account of his experience on the same day, and six days later he learned that Nadezhda had died within minutes of his vision. Moreover, her mother testified that the girl's last words, addressed specifically to the boy, had been, 'There is neither dust nor decay.'

Impressed by the mounting evidence for telepathic phenomena, the 1924 congress resolved that an investigation 'on strictly scientific lines' was called for, and the man who was to devote his life to doing this was one of Bekhterev's students, Leonid L. Vasiliev (1891–1966). He began his career knowing that telepathy existed – because he had experienced it himself. When he was 12 he had nearly drowned after falling into a river. He begged his guardians not to tell his parents, who were 800 miles (1300 kilometres) away, but as soon as his mother came home, she retold the whole story down to the detail of his new white cap being swept away by the current. She had dreamed the whole episode at the time.

Despite this personal experience, Vasiliev embarked objectively on his research into telepathy. He assumed there must be some physical explanation for it, and although he never found one, he did discover a number of practical ways in which telepathy can be made to work. In 1926, he carried out a series of experiments in a Leningrad hospital designed to convey mental suggestions to a hypnotised subject to commit trivial actions such as raising a certain arm or leg or scratching the nose. He was wholly or partly successful 16 times out of 19. Later, after repeating the experiment, he declared that both conscious and unconscious movements of a human body could be caused by mental suggestion alone.

A remote possibility?

And he also found that it was possible to send somebody to sleep or wake them up by a kind of mental remote control, even at distances of up to 1000 miles (1600 kilometres). Moreover, he found that screening the sender inside a Faraday cage (through which almost no form of electromagnetic radiation can pass) had no appreciable effect on his success rate. But Vasiliev failed in his main aim, which was to establish a physical basis for telepathy. His greatest achievement was to provide continuity between the pioneer days of the 1920s and the sudden renaissance of Soviet psi research that began after Khrushchev's historic denunciation of Stalinism in 1956.

Little is known about Vasiliev's research over the latter part of his life, although in 1940, a few months before the siege of Leningrad, he was carrying out experiments in his laboratory there that showed how the muscles of an insect's intestines responded to electrical impulses emitted from contracting human muscles. Such work might not seem a vital part of the Russian war effort, yet it appears that Vasiliev was still determined to find physiological evidence for 'brain power' transference.

Also in 1940, none other than Joseph Stalin himself acted as psychical researcher for a short while, after showing an interest in one of the country's most popular stage performers, telepathist Wolf Messing. According to Messing's story, as published in the official Soviet press (and never officially denied), Stalin put the telepathist's power of mind control to the test by having him persuade a bank clerk that a blank piece of paper was a cheque for 100,000 roubles, then walking unchallenged through the dictator's own security guards after hypnotising them into thinking that he was secret police chief Lavrenty Beria. If his report is true, Messing, who died in the early 1970s, could have been the greatest spy of all time.

However, despite Messing's popularity, and Stalin's private views on the subject, telepathy was defined in the 1956 *Great Soviet encyclopedia* as 'an anti-social, idealist fiction about man's supernatural power to perceive phenomena which, considering the

Above: Wolf Messing (on the right), the popular Soviet stage telepathist. Messing's work attracted the attention of Joseph Stalin

Below: Dr Milan Ryzl, the Czech parapsychologist who fears Vasiliev's best research was kept secret

time and place, cannot be perceived.' Vasiliev's whole life had apparently been spent in vain, at least as far as public recognition was concerned. Yet, after a typically sudden policy reversal, he was allowed to re-enter the field of parapsychology with government backing in 1960, the specific task of his Laboratory of Aero-ions and Electromagnetic Waves at Leningrad University (where he had by then become head of the physiology department) being 'to study the phenomena of telepathy'. He must have felt his life had come full circle after 40 years.

Czech parapsychologist Milan Ryzl has claimed that Vasiliev was almost certainly engaged in secret research, and it seems plausible that it was the prospect of discovering the mechanism of telepathy that kept research funds flowing in. And if ever they did discover it, the Soviet authorities would have in their power a means of domination of which even Lenin could never have dreamed.

Research and experiment in parapsychology is thriving behind the Iron Curtain – and has attracted the interest of security and military officials.

IN 1957, ONLY THREE ARTICLES appeared on the subject of parapsychology in the entire Soviet press, and they were all hostile. Ten years later, the total had risen to 152, and less than 10 per cent were negative or even critical. Psychic matters had become respectable and, as a steady stream of Western journalists soon discovered, there was plenty to write about. All over the Soviet Union, it seemed, talented subjects were demonstrating their paranormal abilities to scientists, who in turn were eager to share their new discoveries with Western colleagues. The Soviets were in fact just as interested in telepathy, psychokinesis, UFOs, paranormal healing, and the rest of the psi spectrum as anybody else.

On the death of Leonid Vasiliev in 1966, a new generation of Soviet researchers, many directly inspired by him, was ready to carry on and expand his work. A young physicist, Viktor Adamenko, was studying the psychokinetic talent of his wife Alla Vingradova. Dr G.A. Sergeyev, a mathematician and neurophysiologist, was deeply involved in research into Man's interactions – both normal and paranormal – with his environment. Biochemist Yuri Kamensky had shown himself to be an unusually successful transmitter of telepathy, and his long-distance experiments

Bottom: the might of Soviet arms. But is the real threat from the East a sinister form of telepathy – mind control?

Below: Dr Genady Sergeyev, a mathematician and neurophysiologist, with his invention, a 'bioenergy measuring device'

with actor Karl Nikolayev fully supported earlier work by Vasiliev. At the Kazakh State University in Alma-Ata, biophysicist Dr V.M. Inyushin was evolving his theory of the human 'bioplasma body' and developing the high-frequency photographic technique rediscovered and popularised by Semyon and Valentina Kirlian.

Their star performers
The scientists had plenty of star performers to work with. Soviet housewife Nina Kulagina was willing to demonstrate her PK abilities to order, whether to scientists in laboratories or to Western visitors in hotel rooms. Rosa Kuleshova was repeatedly proving her ability to read with her fingertips. Boris Yermolayev was satisfying astonished observers, including the eminent psychologist Dr Venyamin Pushkin, that he could levitate objects and even people. A young Azerbaijani named Tofik Dadashev was all set to carry on the stage tradition set by popular telepathist Wolf Messing and bring publicly demonstrated telepathy into almost every city in the country.

Behind all this excitement, the scientists were hard at work on theoretical aspects of psi, led by Dr Ippolit Kogan, head of the newly formed Bioinformation Section of a Moscow technical institute. And although parapsychology had never been recognised as a scientific discipline in its own right, a young biologist named Eduard Naumov was devoting himself to it full-time, determined to increase and improve East-West relations

This is Moscow calling

Bottom left: Dr Viktor Inyushin, a biophysicist at Kazakh State University. His research into Kirlian photography is officially approved by the state

Below right: Soviet actor Karl Nikolayev, the subject of many successful experiments into long-distance telepathy

Viktor Adamenko (above) and Alla Vingradova (right) demonstrate their PK ability for American authors Henry Gris and William Dick during a visit to the USSR. Adamenko is holding a small electric light bulb that spontaneously lit up when placed next to an object that had been acted upon by his wife's psychokinetic abilities. Vingradova moves a metal cigar tube by passing her hand over it. It seems unlikely that this represents the most impressive PK the Soviets can muster

in his chosen field of research.

Elsewhere in Eastern Europe, the psychic scene looked equally promising, especially in Czechoslovakia, where Dr Milan Ryzl was showing that paranormal skills could be aroused by training and the use of hypnosis. Working over a three-year period with a single subject, Pavel Stepanek, he achieved significantly positive results nine times out of ten in card-guessing experiments, several of which were witnessed by Western visitors. He had, he claimed, published details of the first demonstration of repeatable telepathy under laboratory conditions. 'The subject,' he said, 'evidently and repeatedly manifested the faculty of extra-sensory perception.'

Also in Czechoslovakia, engineer-inventor Robert Pavlita aroused considerable interest with his 'psychotronic generators' – small metal objects with which, he claimed, he was able to store 'biological energy'.

Meanwhile, Bulgaria had become the first country in the world to boast a state-run psychic, a blind woman named Vanga Dimitrova from the small southern town of Petrich. Any visitor could walk into the Sofia office of Balkantourist, the state travel agency, and book a sitting with her. He would then drive to Petrich, spend the night in the state hotel built especially for

Dimitrova's clients and sleep with a sugar lump under his pillow. The next day he would visit Dimitrova and, when he reached the head of the queue, she would take the lump from him, press it to her forehead, and immediately reel off a flood of information about his past, present and future. Bulgaria could also boast another world first: its official parapsychology institute in the centre of Sofia, headed by Georgi Lozanov, a medical doctor who, like thousands of other Bulgarians, had received accurate personal information from Dimitrova. He was later to become famous for his method of rapid learning through 'suggestology'.

East-West dialogue

In the 1960s Eastern Europe was indeed the centre of parapsychology. But it was not to last. In 1968, Eduard Naumov organised an international conference in Moscow, which was attended by nine Westerners, including journalists Lynn Schroeder and Sheila Ostrander from the USA. Hardly had the meeting begun when *Pravda* came out with a savage attack on parapsychology in general and PK medium Nina Kulagina in particular; delegates were dismissed from the House of Friendship, and word went round that the East-West dialogue between parapsychologists was over.

Matters were made even worse when Schroeder and Ostrander published *Psychic discoveries behind the Iron Curtain* in 1970. This popular book contained an enormous amount of information on developments in

Eastern Europe and the USSR previously unknown to Westerners, and led to a considerable increase of interest in them. It also made it clear that the Soviets were way ahead of the field in most areas of research into the paranormal. But Soviet authorities did not like the book at all. It was, they said, 'overflowing with factual errors and undisguised anti-Soviet thrusts', and they reacted violently to the suggestion that parapsychology was linked to 'defence, psychological warfare, espionage, etc'.

Reliable observers consider, however, that what really angered the authorities was the indiscretion of Naumov, who had revealed a couple of state secrets: one, that the

Left: PK 'superstar' Nina Kulagina moving a matchbox by telekinesis. Later in 1977, although recovering from a near-fatal heart attack, she repeated this feat during a filmed demonstration in Moscow. Her psychokinesis cost her a tremendous physical effort, unlike that of Western psychics such as Uri Geller or the Philip group in Toronto

Below: Boris Yermolaev demonstrates the 'passes' he makes while paranormally suspending objects in the air

contributions. 'There is no doubt that we are experiencing the birth of a unique science,' said Krippner of the study of psychotronics, 'one which requires a combination of the physical and behavioural sciences with a new, holistic viewpoint on the organisation of life systems.'

A solid bridge had at last, it seemed, been built. Several Westerners visited the Eastern bloc countries, and formed close friendships with their counterparts there. Further psychotronic congresses were held at two-year intervals, and although there was no Soviet presence in Monaco in 1975 or in Tokyo in 1977, a team of Moscow medical researchers attended the 1979 gathering in Brazil, where Dr Rejdak made a firm plea for placing psychotronic research above politics.

One might have thought that Schroeder and Ostrander had closed the door for other

Soviet military had carried out experiments in animal telepathy between a submarine and the shore, and the other, that a method had been devised to intercept telepathy between humans. Both these reports, if true, could have considerable military significance; conventional communication with a submerged submarine can be extremely difficult, and if telepathy were to become a weapon of war, a means of intercepting it would be of the greatest value.

A trumped-up charge

Although Naumov managed to organise another highly successful international meeting in 1972, he was in serious trouble the following year – allegedly for a financial misdemeanour – and was arrested and sentenced to two years' forced labour in March 1974. Perhaps as a result of vigorous international protest, he was released a year later; however, he was not allowed to resume his work and he disappeared altogether from the parapsychological scene.

In October 1973, the Soviet press published an article that seemed, at last, to define the official attitude towards parapsychology and go some way to explaining the USSR's erratic international relations. The message was clear. Psi phenomena did indeed exist – some of them, anyway – and should be researched, but not by amateurs or 'militant individuals' (a clear reference to Naumov), but by the Soviet Academy of Sciences instead.

Normal international relations were apparently resumed when, largely on the initiatives of two psychologists, Dr Stanley Krippner (USA) and Dr Zdenek Rejdak (Czechoslovakia), the first International Conference of Psychotronic Research was held in Prague in 1973 (psychotronics is the Eastern term for parapsychology). More than 400 delegates from 21 countries attended, including a group from the Soviet Academy of Sciences, and several Soviet and Eastern European scientists made important

Western writers, but in 1975 two American reporters from the sensationalist weekly *National Enquirer* were given free access to several Soviet research centres, including some that were off limits even to Soviet journalists. Henry Gris and William Dick were as surprised as anybody else at the privilege they had been granted, and one Soviet scientist speculated that his country's authorities were just as curious about Western advances in parapsychology as Westerners were about theirs. They wanted to find out how advanced they really were, he thought, by studying reactions to what Gris and Dick reported.

Yet, even as they were preparing their book, a bizarre incident took place in June 1977 that seemed to put the clock back to the chilliest period of the cold war of the 1950s. On 11 June, the *Los Angeles Times* correspondent in Moscow, Robert C. Toth, was telephoned by a man named Petukhov and asked to meet him in the street at once. Toth did so, and was handed a document, but before he had time even to glance at it, both men were surrounded by plainclothes police and driven off for lengthy – and presumably

reference in a speech to a form of warfare 'more terrifying' than even nuclear weaponry, and the need for the USA to agree to a ban on it; he gave the impression that he knew the American leaders would know what he meant. Was this a veiled reference to biochemical (germ) warfare or had the Toth affair been a gentle reminder to the West that the Soviets were now in a position to wage psychic warfare?

After visiting the USSR shortly before he went to live in the United States, Milan Ryzl reported on a paradoxical state of affairs there. Parapsychology, he said, was poorly funded, yet there were signs of considerable interest from security and military authorities in possible uses of it. Practical application had always been a characteristic of all communist research, and once it became possible to make practical use of psi, Dr Ryzl concluded, 'there is no doubt that the Soviet Union will do so'.

Western researchers have repeatedly been urged by their Eastern colleagues to ensure that psychic forces are used for peace and for the benefit of humanity. 'There is something about the way they say this,' says one, 'that makes it clear to me that some people have other ideas.'

Top: a selection of the various types of psychotronic generator invented by Robert Pavlita (above) in Czechoslovakia. They can, he claims, store biological energy

Left: American journalists Lynn Schroeder (left) and Sheila Ostrander (right) with Soviet parapsychologist Eduard Naumov in Moscow in 1968 during the First International Conference on Parapsychology, which was organised by Naumov. Ostrander and Schroeder published their discoveries in *Psychic discoveries behind the Iron Curtain* in 1970. The book was swiftly denounced by Soviet authorities

Right: Vanga Dimitrova, Bulgaria's famous blind prophetess. She was the world's first known state-financed psychic; sittings with her could be booked through the Bulgarian state travel agency

very unpleasant – interrogation.

Then a man claiming to be a senior member of the Academy of Sciences promptly appeared, read the document, and announced that it contained an account of recent Soviet discoveries on the physical basis of psi phenomena – something they had sought in vain for half a century – and was a state secret. Toth was soon released, after 13 hours of interrogation by the KGB, and allowed to leave the country.

The incident baffled Western observers as much as it did Toth himself, who had never shown any interest in parapsychology. It was thought at the time that he was merely being warned off any involvement with dissidents, but this is unlikely in view of the fact that he had finished his tour and was due to leave anyway. A more probable explanation is that the whole episode, obviously set up by the authorities, was a clumsy bluff. The Soviets had not solved the psi mystery, but they wanted the West to think they had, and they hoped Toth would report something to this effect to his newspaper.

There was another more alarming theory. In 1973 Brezhnev had made an enigmatic

The Third World War?

One of the most disturbing rumours to arise in the late 20th century is that the Soviets have mastered the art of mass mind control – and that they are already using it.

ASTRAL ESPIONAGE; subliminal propaganda by telepathy; thought-moulding of Western leaders; bioenergy as an anti-personnel weapon; knocking out military equipment and space vehicles with psychokinesis – these are not jottings from a science-fiction writer's notebook but some of the techniques solemnly discussed in two reports compiled in 1972 and 1975 for the US Defense Intelligence Agency (DIA) under the titles 'Controlled offensive behavior – USSR' and 'Soviet and Czechoslovak parapsychology research'. The former was scheduled for declassification only in 1990, but has been obtained under the Freedom of Information Act, and while parts of the documents may strain the credulity of the most avid science-fiction fan, a study of them in conjunction with other published information points to the possibility that the Third World War was well under way by the mid 1970s – and that the West was losing it.

According to the DIA reports, the Soviets had a start of several decades over the West in officially funded research into psychic phenomena, especially telepathy, and their top priority has always been practical application. In other words, while the West was holding psychical research at arm's length, or even arguing it out of existence, the Soviets

Right: Shawn Robbins, American psychic, who has revealed that the US Navy once invited her to take part in a project similar to Stanford Research Institute's remote viewing experiments. There is some evidence that many other psychics in Western countries have at least been approached by their governments as potential subjects in large-scale ESP experiments

Below: an early warning station. But what warning would we have if the USSR were to direct weapons of mind control at us?

were looking for – and finding – ways of making telepathy and psychokinesis (PK) work for them.

However, a 1976 report (allegedly funded by one of the US intelligence agencies) was more cautious. Surveying the published literature on what its authors term 'novel biophysical information transfer' (NBIT) – comprising both telepathy and PK – this study concluded that, although most published material was 'confusing, inaccurate and of little value from a scientific point of

Left: Jack Anderson, US columnist and investigative reporter, who announced in early 1981 that the Pentagon had been training a 'psychic task force' (which he also dubbed the 'voodoo warriors') since 1976. Although he treated the subject lightheartedly, other writers, including senior officers of the US Army, viewed it with grave concern

Above: Thomas E. Bearden, a retired US Army officer with a background in defence systems. He believes that the Soviets possess at least 26 devices that employ psychotronic weaponry, including a machine that can broadcast 'disease patterns' and generate earthquakes. Author Lyall Watson discusses Bearden's ideas in *Lifetide* and finds them 'horribly plausible'

Right: Richard Deacon, the British author of several books on espionage. He devotes a whole chapter of his *The Israeli secret service* to 'psychic espionage'

view', there was good reason to suppose that secret psi research was indeed going on in the Soviet Union, the results of which were intended to be made use of by the military and secret police. One of the authors of the report was later quoted as saying, 'I believe the Soviets are actually building prototype equipment for psychic warfare.'

It became known in 1980, thanks to successful use of the Freedom of Information Act by US journalist Randy Fitzgerald, that the Central Intelligence Agency's involvement in psychic matters could be traced back at least to 1952. In a CIA document dated 7 January of that year, the remarkable claim was made that 'it looks as if . . . the problem of getting and maintaining control over the ESP function has been solved,' and it was recommended that 'suitable subjects' should be trained and put to work as psychic spies. A well-known American psychic, Shawn Robbins, later revealed that she had been invited to take part in a US Navy project along the lines of the remote viewing experiments carried out at Stanford Research Institute (SRI) with artist Ingo Swann and retired police commissioner Pat Price.

Finally, early in 1981, psychic warfare made headlines in the USA when columnist Jack Anderson announced that the Pentagon had been maintaining a secret 'psychic task force' since 1976. 'The brass hats,' he said, 'are indeed dabbling in the dark arts.' Anderson does not seem to have taken the activities of what he calls 'the voodoo warriors' very seriously, yet by a curious coincidence the first of his two columns appeared just after a much more thoroughly researched piece on psychotronic warfare in *Military Review*

(December 1980) – no less than the professional journal of the US Army.

The article, on 'The new mental battlefield', was humorously subtitled 'Beam me up, Spock'. But there was nothing funny in the eight-page text, written by Lieutenant-Colonel J.B. Alexander, a holder of three university degrees who had clearly done his homework. Psychotronic research had been under way for years, he wrote, and its potential use in weaponry had been explored. 'To be more specific,' he went on, 'there are weapons systems that operate on the power of the mind and whose lethal capacity has already been demonstrated.' After a candid and open-minded survey of his subject, he admitted that some would find it ridiculous 'since it does not conform to their view of reality'. However, he added, 'some people still believe the world is flat', and he called for more co-ordinated research into the paranormal, recommending that leaders 'at all levels' should be provided with 'a basic understanding of weapons systems they may encounter in the not-too-distant future'.

A terrifying arsenal

Some indication of just what these weapons might be has been given by Thomas E. Bearden, a retired US Army officer with long experience in nuclear engineering, war games analysis and air defence systems. He describes a terrifying arsenal of some 26 devices, ranging from machines that modify the weather and broadcast 'disease patterns' to the 'hyperspace nuclear howitzer' and even an earthquake generator. Bearden uses quantum mechanics and Jungian psychology to build a model of psychotronic reality that is unlikely to conform to the views of many, although Lyall Watson, who discusses Bearden's theories in his book *Lifetide*, finds some of his ideas 'horribly plausible' and senses 'a rightness in his approach'.

Before the psychotronic scenario gets

even more bizarre, two questions must be asked: who is winning the psi arms race, and is there any real evidence that any psi weaponry has ever been used?

According to Richard Deacon, author of several studies of international espionage, the first country to take the lead in psi warfare techniques could achieve 'something like total superiority'. And, he says, the country with the most active interest in and best information on the subject is neither of the superpowers, but Israel. Quoting intelligence sources, Deacon states that the Israelis have first-hand knowledge of military psi research in seven Russian cities and at least four Eastern European countries. One of the Israelis' most alarming claims is that the Soviets were working in the mid 1970s on 'subliminal conditioning' by telepathy, through 'transference of behaviour impulses'. According to Deacon's source, telepathic mind control had already been put into practice.

In 1976, one possible means by which this could be done became public knowledge. In

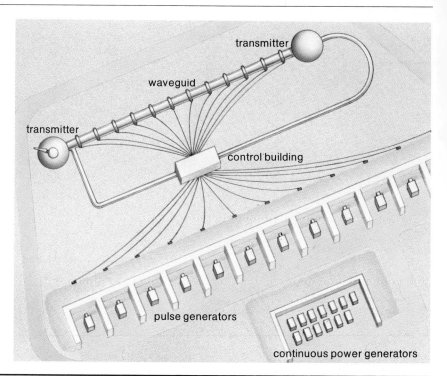

A pawn in their game

Anatoli Karpov, Soviet grand master, and Viktor Korchnoi, the Soviet defector, during their intense battle of wits at the 1978 World Chess Championship at Baguio City in the Philippines

Who really won the 1978 World Chess Championship – Soviet grand master Anatoli Karpov, Soviet defector Viktor Korchnoi, or a mysterious man named Dr Vladimir Zukhar? According to the record books, it was the seemingly unflappable Karpov who retained his title after winning five games out of the first six, losing the next four, and finally returning to form and sweeping the board.

The more volatile Korchnoi thought otherwise. Dr Zukhar, he alleged, was a psychic saboteur sent to Baguio City in the Philippines to make sure that Karpov avoided losing to a defector.

Korchnoi obviously believed that psychic powers could affect his game, for he took countermeasures of his own, in the form of training in yoga and meditation from a couple of American members of the Anand Marg sect who happened to be in town. They also taught him a Sanskrit mantra to ward off evil, which he claimed to have used against Zukhar with devastating effect.

This was not the first time psychic matters had been raised at a world chess tournament. Interestingly, it was the Soviets who cried foul play at the 1972 confrontation between Bobby Fischer and Boris Spassky, suggesting not only that Fischer's chair was wired to receive messages from accomplices, but that Fischer, or at any rate somebody, was actually trying to cast an evil spell over Spassky. And at the world title elimination bout in 1977, Spassky had part of the stage screened off, so that he could hide from both Korchnoi and the audience. The former was paralysing his mind, he said, while the latter were beaming rays at him.

Could Dr Zukhar have helped Karpov win in 1978? By then, the Soviets had more than 50 years of state-backed research in telepathy to draw on, and if scientists in the 1920s could broadcast suggestions that subjects should scratch their noses, it seems possible that Zukhar could make Korchnoi move the wrong pawn at the wrong time.

'Chess is almost the perfect game for PK effects to make a real difference,' says Dr Carl Sargent, a Cambridge parapsychologist and chess enthusiast. 'One lapse of concentration may mean the blunder which costs the game or even the match.' And, he notes, a feature of the Korchnoi-Karpov games in 1978 was the number lost by apparent mistakes rather than won by skill.

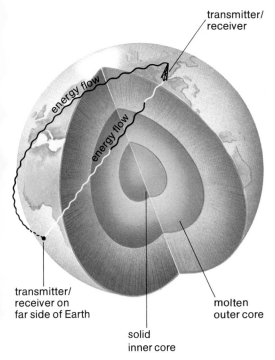

transmitter/
receiver

energy flow

energy flow

transmitter/
receiver on
far side of Earth

molten
outer core

solid
inner core

Left: diagram showing the theoretical application of one of Nikola Tesla's ideas: beaming radio waves through the Earth's core, which would carry psychotronic signals – designed to destroy human brain waves

Far left: diagram of a secret Soviet installation observed at Saryshagan in the USSR. Some observers believe it houses a laser beam weapon or particle beam weapon but Thomas E. Bearden believes it is based on a Tesla invention and can be used to form a 'bubble' of energy – a force field. This could be employed as a defensive shield, or actively, against enemy aircraft

Below: a scene from the 1977 MGM film *Telefon* in which a mad Soviet agent, 'Telefon' (played by Donald Pleasance), activates 'sleepers' using an hypnotic code. They then blow up US military bases

that year, a number of new Soviet radio stations went on the air, mystifying listeners around the world by confining their programme content to a loud and steady rattle. One of these stations, at Gomel (near Minsk), was believed to have 20 times the peak output of any previously known transmitter, and the Soviet 'woodpecker' (which is what it sounded like) was splashing across several frequencies on the short-wave band and even interfering with telephones.

Telecommunications companies, amateur radio societies and several governments complained to the Soviet Union. The Soviets apologised, said they were carrying out 'experiments' and promised to minimise disruption. But they never explained what they were doing, and early guesses were that they were working on a new form of over-the-horizon radar. Then, in November 1977, the American psychical investigator Andrija Puharich startled a London audience with a detailed account of what he believed was really going on. 'It isn't that they are interfering with radio and telephone systems,' he said. 'They are actually interfering with your heads. Somebody, far away, is playing with your minds.' He went on to explain how they were doing it.

The Soviets, he said, had put into practice an idea originally thought up by scientist Nikola Tesla (1857–1943) around the turn of the century, and were using their transmitters to set up a colossal stationary wave passing through the core of the earth and carrying a signal tuned to resonate with the earth–atmosphere system. This signal was being pulsed at frequencies in the extremely low frequency (ELF) band, of 4 to 15 pulses per second, a range of special importance to the human brain, comprising the theta and alpha bands.

In laboratory experiments, Puharich found that brain rhythms fell into step with whatever frequency in these bands was being beamed at them, even when the subject was in a shielded metal Faraday cage. Fine tuning of the pulse rate could produce a wide range of symptoms, from tension headaches to nausea and drowsiness, and this sinister process of 'bioentrainment' was being tried out on the country selected for the Soviet 'experiment' – Canada.

This was not all. Puharich reckoned that ways had been found to get the psychotronic effect, in the form of a telepathic signal, onto the woodpecker signal. Something like this had been specifically predicted in detail by the authors of the 1976 report mentioned above. Therefore, fantastic as it may seem, it is an idea that has occurred to others besides Puharich. It has often been noted that the physicist Dr Ippolit M. Kogan put forward a hypothesis in the 1960s on the use of ELF waves as carriers of telepathy, and that after 1969 Kogan's name completely disappeared from the published literature, nobody in the West hearing any more from him. And Western parascientists noticed that any accounts of psychical research published by the Soviets after 1970 described old, well-known experiments, as if their real work in this field were suddenly deemed top secret.

'Fighting is the most primitive way of making war on your enemies,' wrote the Chinese philosopher Sun Tzu some 2400 years ago. 'The supreme excellence,' he said, 'is to subdue the armies of your enemies without having to fight them.' At the start of the 1980s, it seemed that it would soon be known if any nation had managed to achieve this supreme excellence through psychotronic weaponry, or whether the whole subject of psi warfare was destined to rest where many believed it always belonged – in the realm of science fiction.

Left: lightning striking the surface of the sea. The first primitive life forms probably came about after lightning had fused together elements of the Earth's atmosphere to create the potential for life

Above: fern-like crystals of the amino acid tryptophan – one of the basic 'building blocks' of life

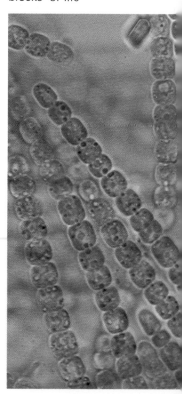

The miracle of life

Established science holds that life came about purely by accident and that it can be explained entirely by the laws of physics and biology. But, as COLIN WILSON explains, there is another, more exciting possibility: could life be a force independent of matter, which somehow controls mechanical processes for a purpose of its own?

ACCORDING TO the theories of modern astronomy, our Universe began about 10 billion years ago with a tremendous explosion. After a billion or so years, great clouds of steamy gas formed into galaxies, and eventually the whirls and eddies in this spinning gas contracted into stars. Until this point, there had been nothing in the Universe but the two 'simplest' gases – hydrogen and helium. But as the stars contracted, the pressure became great enough to crush together these simple atoms to form carbon – the basic building block of life.

But life cannot exist without various heavy elements, such as iron, phosphorus and sulphur, and these were also locked up in the cores of the gigantic stars. Billions more years had to pass, until the original stars grew old, gave off most of their energy in the form of radiation, and collapsed and exploded,

before the essential elements floated free.

And how did life evolve? The usual account is that the various elements – carbon, nitrogen, phosphorus, oxygen, hydrogen, iron – somehow came together in the great witches' cauldron of our cooling planet, were fused together by lightning, and formed complex molecules called amino acids, the basic constituents of all living organisms. But in 1963, astronomers discovered molecules of combined oxygen and hydrogen out in deep space; science calls them 'hydroxyl groups'. A few years later, radio astronomers also discovered water, ammonia, formaldehyde and methyl alcohol in space. No one is quite sure how these atoms came to be formed, but they could have come into existence in outer space and been brought to Earth by comets as Fred Hoyle has argued.

And now we come to the more difficult

and controversial part of the story. How did this dead matter turn into life? The standard account is that the organic molecules found their way into the oceans and, over millions more years, accidental collisions formed every conceivable shape and size of molecule. And finally, a molecule was formed that had the amazing power to reproduce itself.

But there are problems in this explanation. Life begins with 'protein chains', each made up of many amino acids, with 20 possibilities for each link in the chain. In his book *Human destiny* the French biophysicist Lecomte de Noüy pointed out that, even if a new combination were tried every millionth of a second, it would still take longer than the lifetime of our Earth to form a chain associated with life – the odds against it being a one followed by 95 zeros.

In 1953 the American scientist Stanley Miller conducted an experiment in which electrical discharges – artificial lightning – were passed through a mixture of water, ammonia, methane and hydrogen, the substances that were believed to have formed the primitive atmosphere of the Earth. At the end of a day, the mixture turned pink; at the end of a week, Dr Miller found that two of the simplest amino acids had been formed. The latest findings of modern research suggest that the early atmosphere of the Earth was in fact made up of carbon dioxide and water vapour. But, when Dr Miller's experiment was repeated using carbon dioxide and water, similar results were obtained – again, simple amino acids were formed.

Alternative theory of life

So it seems that the Earth's primitive atmosphere, lightning and chance could together have produced the building blocks of life. But this still leaves unanswered Lecomte de Noüy's objection that it would take thousands of billions of years for these acids to form a protein chain, Still, scientists can take comfort from the notion that there seem to be 'natural laws' that favour the formation of living cells.

An alternative theory about life *has* been in existence for over two centuries. It was conceived one day in 1762, when an Italian professor of anatomy named Luigi Galvani was studying amputated frogs' legs on a bench in his laboratory. (Legend has it that they were waiting to be made into soup!) On a nearby bench, someone was turning the handle of an electrical machine. Galvani happened to touch one of the frogs' legs with a metal scalpel – and, to his surprise, it 'kicked'. What had happened, it seemed, was that the electric sparks caused a 'wave' of electricity, which was picked up by the scalpel; this, in turn, transmitted it to a nerve – which behaved just as if the frog's brain had ordered the leg to move. This seemed to imply that the brain gives its orders by electrical telegraph. In fact, Galvani's observation led to the discovery that human beings *are* electrical machines; every time we think, the brain discharges electric currents.

Late last century, a young biologist named Hans Driesch tried an experiment with the fertilised egg of a sea urchin. He waited until it divided, then killed off one half with a hot needle. To his surprise, the surviving half did not turn into 'half' a sea urchin; it developed into a perfect but smaller embryo of a whole sea urchin. Clearly, each half of the egg contained a 'blueprint' of the whole.

He tried pressing two eggs together; they fused and developed into a larger than normal embryo.

Driesch argued, sensibly, that organisms can only be understood as living *wholes*, not as machines made up of bits and pieces. That, nowadays, sounds unexceptionable. What upset Driesch's contemporaries was that he went on to suggest that if organisms

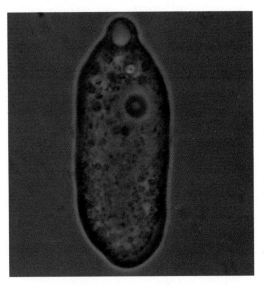

had a purpose, then the 'purpose' must be quite separate from their 'mechanical' parts – the biological bits and pieces, so to speak. In other words, the life in a living creature is something quite separate from its chemistry. Driesch's scientific contemporaries were indignant. They growled 'vitalist' or 'mystic', and ignored him.

Still, not all scientists were obsessed by the idea of explaining nature in purely mechanistic terms. Across the Atlantic another professor of anatomy, Harold Saxton Burr of Yale University, was deeply interested in Driesch's ideas – particularly in the notion that cells contain a 'blueprint'. The first thing he wanted to examine was the electrical forces that seem to set the whole thing in motion. The problem, of course, is that these currents are so tiny that they are very difficult to measure. Burr was not discouraged; together with a colleague, F. S. C. Northrop, he developed methods of attaching a voltmeter to trees – and other living organisms – and keeping a continuous record of their voltages. The trees showed a regular seasonal variation in voltage, which also varied with sunspot activity and phases of the Moon;

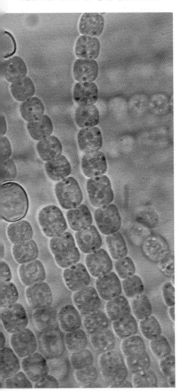

The 'mechanical' argument for evolution runs into difficulties when faced with primitive organisms like the amoeba (right: *Saccamoeba limax*, magnified 500 times) and blue-green alga (below: *Anabaena*, magnified 180 times). No one knows how the simple cell of the alga could evolve into the complex nuclear cell of the amoeba

when the voltmeter was attached to a rabbit's ovary, it showed a sudden jump in voltage as the follicle ruptured, releasing the egg. It was discovered that this technique could be used to help women who were having difficulty becoming pregnant. When the voltmeter was attached to mental patients, it showed quite clearly who were the most 'disturbed'. It could also record the ups and downs in physical illness – for example, to detect cancer at an early stage.

Burr's experiments confirmed him in his conclusion that all living organisms are influenced by their electric fields – he called them L-fields (life fields) for short. If a salamander embryo is placed in an alkaline solution, its individual cells 'disaggregate', or separate; but if these are then placed back in a slightly acid solution, they come together again and re-form into an embryo. Burr compared this to what happens when a magnet is held underneath iron filings on a sheet of paper – they form into a pattern. And he concluded that the 'blueprint' of life is contained in the L-field, which causes the cells to come together into a certain shape. A frog's egg shows various lines of electrical force; when it develops into a tadpole, these lines turn out to be its nervous system. The electric field seems to be a kind of jelly-mould into which the living matter is poured.

In the late 1930s, a Russian professor, Semyon Kirlian, made a discovery that seems to support Burr's theory. When living matter – anything from a human hand to a leaf – was photographed between high-voltage metal plates, the photograph showed the object surrounded by a kind of glowing corona. When a newly-cut flower was photographed, it showed sparks flowing from the stem. It looked very much as if Professor Kirlian had succeeded in photographing the L-field – although sceptical scientists continue to insist that this is just a freak effect due to irregularities in the high-voltage current. Perhaps the most exciting of Kirlian's experiments involved a torn leaf; the photograph appeared to show the *missing* portion of the leaf in dim outline. Unlike Burr's experiments, those of Kirlian are still a matter of violent disagreement among

scientists; but many respected experimenters are convinced that Kirlian discovered how to photograph the 'fields of life'.

Of course, all this does not *prove* Driesch's 'vitalism'. It only proves his assertion that life seems to aim at 'wholeness'. And the controversial word here is 'aim'. Scientists do not like words implying purpose; they prefer to believe that life 'aims' at wholeness only in the same sense that a snowflake 'aims' at getting to the ground. But new discoveries are continually upsetting their old mechanistic models.

An odd kind of 'freedom' was demonstrated, for example, in experiments conducted at the University of Wisconsin in the

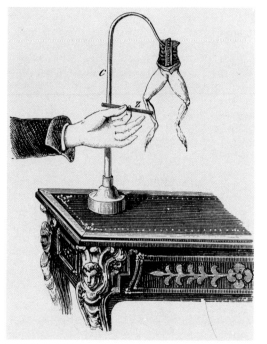

mid-1970s by Daniel Perlman and Robert Stickgold. They grew bacteria in a solution containing an antibiotic that would normally destroy it; the bacteria used has a gene that can produce an enzyme to destroy the antibiotic, so it *can*, in fact, survive. But according to the mechanistic view, it should do this by 'switching on' its defence system, then switching it off when the danger has passed. In fact, the bacteria reacted by making vast numbers of copies of the protective gene – as if the bacteria had decided to *choose* a more reliable defence policy.

Professor C.H. Waddington has made a suggestion that comes very close to Burr's 'vital blueprint' – that life may be a matter of rhythms and vibrations, like the patterns that develop on a glass plate strewn with sand if you stroke it with a violin bow. He even suggests life may develop like a musical composition – as an ordered series of vibrations. (Cancer is a disease of disorganisation.)

At the moment, all these exciting ideas are very much in the melting pot; the slag has not settled to the bottom and the scum has not floated to the top. Yet the suggestion that is

Top left: Luigi Galvani (1737–1798), whose famous experiment with frogs' legs in 1762 (left) suggested that the brain gives its orders by electrical impulses

Above: Semyon Kirlian, the Russian scientist who succeeded in photographing what appear to be the life-fields of living organisms

Below: Hans Driesch (1867–1941), the biologist who stressed that each organism must be understood as a living whole and argued that the life force is quite independent of chemistry

beginning to emerge is clear enough. Perhaps life, after all, is not just a 'product' of matter as heat is a product of fire; perhaps it is an organising principle *beyond* matter. In other words, once chance and the laws of nature had formed the basic building blocks – the amino acids – life intervened to organise them into more complex forms.

This view is known as *vitalism*, and most respectable biologists would shudder and turn away at the very idea. Bernard Shaw expressed this view well when he said that life permeates the Universe, and is striving to gain a foothold in matter. The philosopher T.E. Hulme believed that the process of evolution can be described as the insertion of more and more freedom into matter – so that the amoeba could be regarded as a small 'leak' of freedom, while man is a larger leak.

Astonishing consequences

And here we come to the heart of the matter. Science does not recognise the word 'freedom'. Science deals with mechanical procedures. If you say that you have done something of your own free will, the scientist can produce a thousand reasons to prove that you *had* to do it, as a river has to flow downhill. If you reply that *you* can decide whether to contradict him or not, or whether to go off and do something more rewarding, he will tell you that your freedom of thought is also an illusion. If you decline to accept this, then you are opting for the view that life – or freedom – somehow stands *above* matter and mechanism.

If this heretical notion is true, the consequences for science are astonishing. If life is a mere product of matter – as heat is of burning – then life is a slave of matter. But if it somehow exists separately, then it is potentially the master. This means, in effect, that life (or mind) could overrule the laws of nature. And there is a name for this ancient belief: it is called magic.

This is the question with which science will one day have to come to terms: whether the Universe is basically 'magical'. Some scientists are willing to concede that it probably is. For example, a cybernetician named David Foster has made a study of the 'programming' of DNA, and has concluded that Darwinian biology is probably mistaken. Cybernetics is the study of systems of control – like a thermostat, which switches off the heat when the room gets above a certain temperature. One of the basic laws of cybernetics says that a man who devises such a system must always be more intelligent than the system itself; in other words, a programmer must always be more intelligent than the system he programmes, no matter how high the 'artificial intelligence' of that system.

Now a gene is, in fact, a programme. And it is Foster's contention that the complexity of our genetic programming indicates higher energies and higher intelligences than anything we can find on Earth. Which suggests very definitely that man is not the highest intelligence in the Universe. There *must*, says Foster, be higher intelligences 'out there'. Perhaps the Universe itself is one vast intelligence . . .

When we move into these realms, we are coming alarmingly close to certain questions that are ignored by the majority of scientists – questions, for example, about the 'paranormal', about UFOs, about other dimensions of space and time. At the beginning of his book *Lifetide*, the zoologist Lyall Watson claims that he watched a small girl stroke a tennis ball, and – incredibly – saw the ball turn itself inside out, without breaking its surface. Impossible. But in a universe with even one extra dimension of reality, it could be as commonplace as turning a glove inside out. And if life is not a product of matter, but somehow exists 'beyond' it, our Universe *has* that magical level, and cannot be described in purely physical terms.

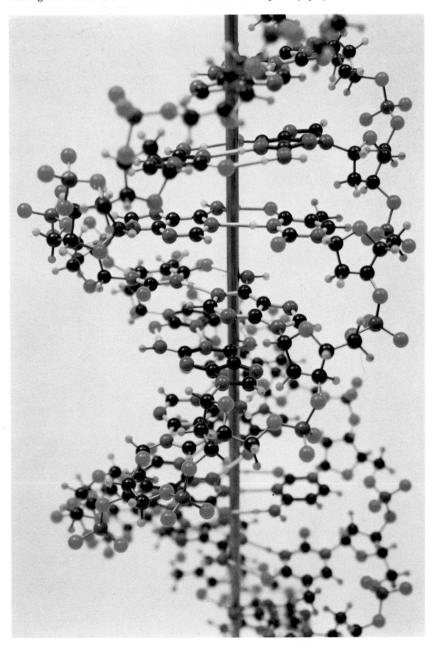

Below: a model of the double helix of DNA, which carries the genetic code of living beings. Cybernetician David Foster has argued that the quality of our genetic programming may indicate that it was designed by a being with a higher intelligence than that of Man

The dead can be restored to a semblance of life – as zombies, the mindless slaves of evil magicians. So the superstitious people of Haiti, steeped in voodoo tradition, believe. FRANK SMYTH examines the tales that are told of the zombies' dreadful fate

'NEAR HER, THE BLACK FINGERS of one silent guest were clutched rigidly around the fragile stem of a wine glass, tilted, spilling. The horror pent up in her overflowed. She seized a candle, thrust it close to the slumped, bowed face, and saw the man was dead. She was sitting at a banquet table with four propped-up corpses. . . .'

So concluded the account of a voodoo wedding breakfast held in the 1920s and recounted to the American journalist William Seabrook by his Haitian friends. The corpses were intended to be turned by sorcery into zombies – half-animate bodies living a twilight existence as the slaves of the magician who was the banquet's host. (In fact, according to Seabrook, his intention was thwarted, he fled and the corpses disappeared.)

There is only one country in the Western world where such a ghastly celebration might have taken place: Haiti, birthplace of voodoo.

Do voodoo sorcerers really have the power to reanimate newly dead corpses? Or is the notion of the zombie pure self-deception on the part of voodoo practitioners?

The word *zumbi* appears in many African languages. In the Congo it means a fetish; in Dahomey it refers specifically to the Python God. In modern voodoo it seems that a snake deity is called upon to animate the zombie at the whim of the sorcerer who has become the corpse's master. The rites involved combine aspects of African magic and religion, with elements derived from both Western occultism and popular Catholicism.

Voodoo played its part in the revolution in which Haitians threw off French rule. In August 1791 France was in the throes of the turmoil that had begun some two years previously. The King and Queen were prisoners, the nobility and clergy had seen their power torn from them, and liberty, equality and fraternity had been adopted as the watchwords of the new order.

Little seemed at first to have changed in St Domingue, the western third of the Caribbean island of Hispaniola, the brightest jewel in the French colonial crown. There, 40,000 Frenchmen controlled half a million black slaves and 30,000 mulattos, growing crops of cotton, sugar, coffee and indigo. The first effect of the disturbances in France had been to improve the lot of the mulattos. Then the darker-skinned Haitians grew restless, helped by the agitation of a mysterious priest-sorcerer named Boukman who had

Above: the role of a zombie is acted out in a voodoo street festival. The whitened face and shroud-like wrappings suggest a newly buried corpse

Below: the structures over these Haitian graves are intended to make them into secure homes for the corpses. Even the poor spend large sums on fortifying their graves

More dead than alive

found his way to St Domingue from the British colony of Jamaica. On 14 August 1791 Boukman summoned those who wished to follow him to a rendezvous deep in the forests. According to contemporary accounts, thousands of slaves slipped away along secret forest trails to the meeting, during a colossal tropical storm that must have lent extra terror and awe to the proceedings that followed.

Boukman conducted a blood ritual, sacrificing a pig and asking all who wished to be free to drink of the still-warm blood. The ceremony ended with a wild dance of 'divine inebriation', after which the participants melted away into the forests again. The whole ritual closely resembled the activities of Mau Mau during the Kenyan war of independence of the 1950s – and it had a similar result. During the next few days most of the great plantations were overrun and their owners killed. Although the stronger French colonists clung on for a further 12 years, the final result of the nocturnal gathering was the complete defeat of the French and the establishment, under the leadership of President Toussaint l'Ouverture, of the independent black republic of Haiti – home of voodoo. And, according to the beliefs of the Haitian peasantry and, often enough, of the educated élite, it was also the home of the zombie, that sinister, animated, but soulless corpse.

The zombie is the slave of an evil sorcerer, known as a *bokor*, who has removed a newly dead body from its grave and, by means of spells, endowed it with the shadow of life. It is an incomplete existence. Although the zombie eats, breathes, excretes, hears and even speaks, it has no memory of its previous life and no understanding of its own true condition. In other words a zombie is a

Below: the first black ruler of Haiti, Toussaint L'Ouverture, who, though born a slave, became a rebel general and expelled occupying French, Spanish and British forces from his country. Years of turmoil and poverty followed, during which voodoo, a religion of African origin, flourished and satisfied the emotional needs of the Haitian people

Bottom: a dark hat and suit, draped over a gravestone, represent the funereal clothes of Baron Samedi, a voodoo god of death. Paradoxically, the Baron is fond of jesting and ribaldry

fleshly robot, a biological machine.

The Haitian peasant, ever alert for evil or dangerous aspects of voodoo, has several signs by which he can spot a zombie. It tends to lurch from side to side as it walks, to carry out other physical actions in a mechanical way, to have glazed and unfocused eyes, and to have a nasal quality in its voice. This characteristic is particularly associated with death in Haitian folklore, probably because it is the local custom to plump out the nostrils of a corpse with cotton wool. The *Guédé* – sinister, lecherous gods of death in the voodoo pantheon – are notable for speaking in this way. When a voodoo devotee is possessed by one of the *Guédé*, he or she always speaks with a strongly nasal intonation. A further link between zombies and the death gods is suggested by the fact that one of the most prominent of the latter, Captain Guédé, is often given the title Captain Zombie.

Almost all Haitians fear the possibility of their deceased relatives being transformed into walking cadavers. The various preventive measures taken to avoid this possibility are readily noticeable in present-day Haiti. For instance, even the poorest peasants will borrow money to build heavy stone coverings over the graves of their immediate relatives. In rural areas graves are dug as near a public road or footpath as possible, so that sorcerers will be unable, for fear of prying eyes, to go about their nefarious work. Sometimes the bereaved family will watch over a new grave for night after night until they are certain that the body is sufficiently decomposed to be useless for the purposes of a *bokor*. On occasion the dead are buried in the

safety of a peasant farm's compound.

Those who particularly dread sorcery carry out even more extraordinary precautions to prevent their dead entering the zombie's misty half-world. They may inject poison into the body, or mutilate it with a knife, or fire a bullet into it, thus 'killing' it twice over.

A less drastic measure is to place eyeless needles and balls of yarn in the grave, along with thousands of tiny sesame seeds. It is thought that the spirit of the dead person will be so busy with the impossible tasks of threading the needle and counting the seeds that it will be unable to hear the voice of a *bokor* calling it from the tomb. Or a knife may be placed in the corpse's hand, with which it can defend itself.

Sorcerers sometimes control whole troops of zombies and on occasion have gone so far as to hire them out as labourers. One alleged case was recorded by William Seabrook.

There was a bumper sugar crop in 1918. Hasco, the Haitian-American Sugar Corporation, offered a bonus for new workers on its extensive plantations. Soon little groups of villagers, including whole families, made their way to the company's labour office. It was customary for such village groups to work collectively, the pay for the entire work force being given to a foreman who shared it out when the party returned home.

One morning an old village headman, Ti Joseph, and his wife Croyance led a band of nine ragged and shuffling men into the Hasco office. They were, explained Joseph, backward and ignorant hill farmers from the trackless mountain area near Haiti's border with the Dominican Republic. They spoke only an obscure rural dialect and could understand neither Creole nor French. In spite of this disadvantage, he continued, they were excellent workmen, strong and healthy, who would labour happily.

Hasco's labour manager took the gang on, agreeing with Joseph's suggestion that they

should work far from other groups: the head man explained that they were so primitive that they would become shy and confused near other people. But his real reason for insisting on his workers' isolation was his fear that one or other of them would be recognised by a relative or former friend. For every one of Ti Joseph's work gang was a zombie.

Ti Joseph's strange labourers worked steadfastly through the hours of daylight, stopping only at dusk for their meal of unsalted millet porridge. Voodoo tradition holds that if a zombie tastes meat or salt it becomes conscious of its true condition and,

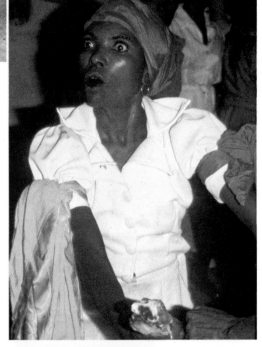

Above left: the African roots of voodoo. The headless body of a sacrificial goat lies on the floor of a hut in Dahomey. The young woman, possessed by the goat's spirit, imitates it by going on all fours. Identical rituals are performed in Haiti

Left: a voodoo priestess, her eyes staring, in the grip of religious frenzy. She has just bitten the head from a chicken: its blood stains her dress

Below left: a machete and the national flag featured in a ceremony in which Haitians honoured the American writer William Seabrook in the 1920s

weeping bitter tears, makes its way back to the grave that is its proper home.

One Sunday morning Ti Joseph left his wife Croyance to look after the zombies while he took the day off. Croyance led them into the nearby town: there was to be a church festival and she apparently thought, surprisingly, that the zombies would be pleased to witness a religious procession. But the zombies were as unmoved by the spectacle as by anything else that happened around them. Dumbly and vacantly they continued to stare into space.

Croyance, pitying them, decided that sweetmeats might please them. She bought some *tablettes*, which are made of brown sugar, coriander and peanuts. She put a piece into each zombie's mouth. But the peanuts had been salted before the *tablettes* had been made. As they chewed the delicacy, the zombies realised that they were dead, that they did not belong to Haiti's bright sunlit world, but to the darkness of the tomb.

With an appalling outcry they rose and shuffled out of the town into the forests and towards their home village in the mountains.

When at last they arrived there, they were recognised by the relatives and friends who had buried them months before. As they reached the graveyard each approached its own grave, scrabbled away the stones and earth that covered it, and then fell to the ground, a mass of corruption. Ti Joseph's power, which had preserved their bodies from decay, had vanished.

The villagers inflicted their revenge on Ti Joseph. They paid a local sorcerer to cast a spell on him. But before it could take its effect, some of the men had ambushed him and cut off his head.

Seabrook was told this tale by Constant Polynice, a Haitian farmer who claimed to disbelieve the superstitions of his countrymen – but the zombies, he explained, were plain fact. Shortly after telling this story, he showed Seabrook a group of three supposed zombies. They were digging with machetes, under the supervision of a young woman. Seabrook looked into the face of one of the men:

> and what I saw then, coupled with what I had heard previously, or despite it, came as a rather sickening shock. The eyes were the worst. It was not my imagination. They were in truth like the eyes of a dead man, not blind, but staring, unfocused, unseeing. The whole face . . . seemed not only expressionless, but incapable of expression.

Seabrook reassured himself that these men were 'nothing but poor ordinary demented human beings, idiots, forced to toil in the fields'. But his Haitian friend was not convinced.

Writing in the 1950s the French anthropologist Alfred Métraux heard a good deal of

Above: in an Haitian temple an altar carrying such Christian images as the Virgin Mary, a crucifix and the Ten Commandments is also adorned with drums, swords and ritual drinking cups – implements used in voodoo ceremonies

Left: this woman, the photographer believed, had been a zombie for 29 years. She had been identified by at least two people as a relative, Felicia Felix-Mentor, who had died in 1907. She was being cared for in a hospital when the journalist Zora Hurston took the picture

evidence both for and against the existence of zombies. But when he was shown one in the flesh he concluded that she was 'a wretched lunatic'. Indeed the following day the person he had seen was identified as a mentally deficient girl who had escaped from the locked room in which she was kept.

A writer who was perhaps less credulous than Seabrook concerning Haitian voodoo was Zora Hurston, another American. She met and photographed a girl who was alleged to have been a zombie for no less than 29 years. In 1907 Felicia Felix-Mentor had died of a sudden illness, and had been buried by her husband and brother. In 1936 a girl dressed only in a thin, torn cotton smock was found wandering in the roadway near the brother's farm. She appeared to have lost the power of speech completely. Felicia's father and brother both identified her as the long-dead girl. Taken to a hospital, she cringed fearfully when anyone approached, as if expecting ill-treatment. It was there that Zora Hurston took her picture and tried to speak to her. Afterwards she wrote:

> The sight was dreadful. That blank face with the dead eyes. The eyelids were white all around the eyes as if they had been burned with acid. There was nothing you could say to her or get from her except by looking at her, and the sight of this wreckage was too much to endure for long.

Could Felicia Felix-Mentor's father and brother have made such confident identification so many years after her burial? Was the girl who had been found merely a wandering lunatic? The firmly entrenched belief of the Haitians that relatives and loved ones have been seen after their burial, living the half-life of the zombie, throws doubt on this comforting theory. Could there be something deeper to the legend of the zombie?

The fear of being raised from the grave as a zombie has afflicted Haiti's rulers and prosperous, educated classes as well as the common people. But the zombies that witnesses have described may never have been truly dead

THE GREAT DIFFICULTY facing any present-day enquirer into any aspect of Haitian life, and especially voodoo, is that for almost 14 years the country was in the grip of one of the cruellest dictatorships in history. François Duvalier – 'Papa Doc' to his friends and his enemies alike – hated and distrusted anything that smacked of the old colonial days. After he had made himself President for life, he barred American, French and British business and political activity in his country. Black himself, he became a scourge to the

peasants and many middle-class people believed him to be godlike and all-powerful. His son 'Baby Doc', although he is also President for life, appears to have relaxed some of his father's restrictions – mainly in the interests of trade – but the all-pervasive influence of the voodoo creed runs too deep to loosen its grip easily. Any foreigner seeking information under these circumstances, therefore, must necessarily sift the wheat from the chaff with care.

Yet there remain tales and snippets of fact that must give even the most hardened sceptic pause for thought. For instance, it was thought for years that Papa Doc was being purely cynical in his exploitation of voodoo 'power'. He himself, it was said, being an educated man, knew the whole thing to be nonsense. In fact, since his death in 1971 his large blue and cream mausoleum, surmounted by a Christian cross, perpetually surrounded by fresh flowers, and standing in

In the midst of life...

thousands of Haitian businessmen of mixed blood.

Papa Doc boasted of being a powerful *bokor* – sorcerer. His personal bodyguard, always masked by dark glasses and laden with arsenals of small arms, were named *tontons macoutes* after the travelling sorcerers who were the most feared figures of voodoo. Papa Doc encouraged the belief in voodoo and in his own magic powers, so that the

the best quarter of Port-au-Prince, has been guarded day and night by armed men. No *bokor* 'working with both hands' – that is, no black magician – is going to steal the Duvalier corpse and turn it into a zombie.

A correspondent for the African magazine *Drum* who visited Haiti in the late 1960s summed up the generally ambivalent attitude of the authorities to voodoo in this way:

A tourist, particularly a journalist, will

Above: the corpse of François Duvalier – 'Papa Doc'. Dictator of Haiti for nearly 14 years, he was a practising Roman Catholic – and also, according to rumour, a practitioner of voodoo sorcery

Below: the tomb of Papa Doc, under continuous armed guard to prevent its desecration – and, perhaps, to deter the activities of voodoo magicians

generally find no difficulty in getting himself invited to a *houmfort* (voodoo temple) in the forest for a Saturday night ceremony. The *hungan* (voodoo priest) and his followers apparently go into trances and dance ecstatically, and everything is very colourful. But mention zombies, or the *Culte des mortes*, which centres on Baron Samedi and worships in graveyards, and one draws a blank. I was convinced that dark practices and secret ceremonies do go on simply by the vehemence of authority's denial that they ever existed at all.

Voodoo has always been big business, and it is not only visiting journalists who are duped. Fraud is frequently uncovered. The British anthropologist Francis Huxley tells how a magistrate watched while a *hungan* took a body from a grave, muttered invocations over it, shook it and finally reanimated

Above: *Les zombies*, a painting by an Haitian artist, Hector Hippolyte, who was himself a voodoo priest. Here two reanimated corpses are driven from the grave to a half-life of servitude by a sorcerer

it. The magistrate, less fearful than his fellows, searched the empty 'tomb' and found a breathing tube leading from it. The 'corpse' had been the *hungan*'s accomplice.

But fraud cannot account for all the disturbing tales told of the zombies. One of these stories was recounted to Huxley by a Catholic priest. In 1959 a zombie was found wandering in a village street. He was taken to the police station, but the police cautiously declined to take any action and he was left standing outside. After some hours he was given a drink of salt water – to restore, at least in part, his mental functioning. The zombie stammered out a name that someone recognised as belonging to a woman living in the village. She was brought, and identified the zombie as her nephew, who had died and

been buried in 1955. The Catholic priest heard of what had occurred, interviewed the zombie, and discovered the name of the *bokor* who had bewitched him. The priest reported the name to the police but they, thoroughly alarmed by now, simply sent a message to the *bokor*, offering him his stray zombie back. Two days later the zombie was found murdered; the *bokor* was arrested, but eventually released.

Alfred Métraux seemed tentatively satisfied with the witnesses to another case of zombie possession dating from the 1950s. A young girl had rejected the sexual advances of a *hungan* who 'worked with both hands'. A few days after she had sent away her unwanted suitor, she fell ill of a high fever and died in hospital of an unspecified complaint. The girl's body was taken home, where a coffin, bought ready-made in Port-au-Prince, had been prepared for its reception. Unfortunately, it proved too short for its intended occupant, and the girl's neck had to be violently bent before the corpse would fit.

A further mishap occurred during the funeral 'wake' in which dancing and rum featured prominently. A lighted candle that illuminated the open casket fell onto the corpse, severely burning the left foot.

Scars of the coffin

A few months after the burial a rumour spread that the supposedly dead girl had been seen in the company of the *hungan* she had rejected. Her family regarded this tale as no more than superstitious gossip. No doubt, they reasoned, the *hungan* was attracted to women of the deceased daughter's physical type and he had acquired a mistress with a slight resemblance to her.

A few years later, however, a son of the family saw a woman who resembled his dead sister working at a menial task. He asked her what her name was. She was unable to say, nor did she have any memory of her past. But her neck was twisted and she bore the scar of a severe burn on her left foot.

She was taken back to her supposed parents' home, but despite loving care she was unable to give a satisfactory account of herself and remained a virtual idiot until her (second?) death.

Another well-authenticated account was reported by the writer Stephen Bonsal in 1912:

> A man . . . fell ill. He had at intervals a high fever, which physicians could not reduce. He had joined a foreign mission church, and the head of this mission visited him. On his second visit this clergyman saw the patient die . . . and helped dress the dead man in his grave-clothes. The next day he assisted at the funeral, closed the coffin lid, and saw the dead man buried.
>
> The mail rider to Jacmel found some days later a man dressed in grave-clothes tied to a tree, moaning. He

freed the poor wretch, who soon recovered his voice but not his mind. He was subsequently identified by his wife, by the physician who had pronounced him dead, and by the clergyman. The recognition was not mutual, however. The victim recognised no-one, and his days and nights were spent moaning inarticulate words no-one could understand. President Nord Alexis placed him on a government farm, near Gonaives, where he was cared for.

A counterfeit death?

Is there a rational, non-supernatural explanation of these and similar cases of 'corpses' being buried and then, months or years later, being found, still alive but mindless? Among those who have thought so was Dr Antoine Villiers, a distinguished French physician who practised medicine in Haiti for many years. He did not believe that anyone had ever been literally raised from the dead; but he was by no means sure, he told the journalist William Seabrook, that some men and women, seeming idiots who toiled in the fields, had not been 'dragged from the actual graves in which they lay in their coffins, buried by their mourning families'.

Villiers was suggesting that some Haitian sorcerers knew of drugs that could induce a coma so deep as to be mistaken for death, and after 'death' and burial, the victim of the poisons could be restored to life – but not, it would seem, to health, for the brain's functioning and memory suffered permanent impairment.

There is some evidence that knowledge of such drugs existed throughout the parts of West Africa from which most slaves were imported, and also, to a lesser extent, in the Caribbean countries inhabited by people descended from slaves: Haiti, Jamaica and elsewhere.

For example, A.W. Cardinall, who had spent many years in the Gold Coast (now Ghana), reported in 1927 that youths of certain tribes often underwent a sort of temporary death. When a youth wished to enter one of the tribe's secret societies, he would be initiated by being cut with a knife. 'Medicine' was inserted into the wounds, producing a prolonged coma. 'He dies for five days' was the expression used by Cardinall. At the end of the five days the youth was given another medicine and restored to healthy life.

It is clear that the knowledge of 'medicines' of the sort used in this rite was taken to the Americas by slaves who were skilled in the magic of their homeland. In 1789 evidence was given to a British government committee on slavery that 'slave sorcerers' impressed strangers with their magical powers by 'showing them a Negro apparently dead who, by dint of their art, soon recovers'.

Further details of this 'raising from the dead' were given by the English writer Monk Lewis, who witnessed the procedure a century and a half ago. The sorcerer sprinkles various powders over the devoted victim, blows upon him, and dances around him, obliges him to drink a liquor prepared for the occasion, and

A doll used in Haitian black magic. It represents the person on whom the sorcerer wishes to cast a spell – from personal malice or merely because he has been paid to do so by some enemy of the victim

In the heat of the moment

Voodoo ritual and the techniques of brainwashing were linked by the distinguished medical psychologist William Sargant. Brainwashing involves subjecting prisoners to prolonged and intense stress, physical and mental exhaustion, and the incessant suggestion of desired attitudes and beliefs. Victims

may strongly resist the beliefs they are required to adopt, but a point is invariably reached at which they break down. As they recover, they enthusiastically espouse the doctrines of their captors, to whom they often feel devotion and love.

Sargant claimed that the dramatic conversions of people listening to Christian 'hell-fire' preachers were due to the stress of religious terror and exaltation, combined with fatigue. And in voodoo ritual, rhythmic drumming and chanting, exhaustion, and the fear of sinister gods could similarly result, he believed, in a personality shift, when participants are 'possessed' (left), mimicking skilfully the behaviour of some god. At least one visiting anthropologist, caught up in the frenzied dancing, experienced a 'spiritual rebirth', followed by 'agreement with, and admiration for, the principles and practice' of voodoo. Such powerful processes of suggestion may account for the strength of Haitians' belief in voodoo deities, the powers of magicians – and the reality of zombies.

finally the sorcerer and his assistant seize him and whirl him rapidly round and round till the man loses his senses, and falls to the ground, to all appearances and the belief of the spectators a perfect corpse. The chief . . . then utters loud shrieks, rushes out of the house with frantic gestures, and conceals himself in a neighbouring wood. At the end of two or three hours, he returns with a large bundle of herbs, from some of which he squeezes the juice into the mouth of the dead person; with others he anoints his eyes, and stains the tips of his fingers, accompanying the ceremony with a great variety of grotesque actions, and chanting all the while something between a song and a howl. . . . A considerable time elapses before the desired effect is produced, but at length the corpse gradually recovers animation, [and] rises from the ground. . . .

The plant that was reputed to produce the state of cataleptic trance was called *callaloo*. If it was so used, it must have been prepared in a special way, or acquired its powers by being compounded with drugs, for *callaloo* is of itself quite harmless and indeed is sometimes boiled to a pulp and eaten as a vegetable.

Belladonna and thorn apple are two vegetable poisons believed by ordinary Haitians to be blended with more magical substances – for example, three drops of fluid from a corpse's nose – to make the medicines by which sorcerers control zombies.

In fact a number of drugs are known to

Right: the gravestone of a 'voodoo queen' – Marie Laveau, a priestess. This memorial is in an American outpost of voodoo – New Orleans, the great Mississippi port. Voodoo worshippers would come to the tomb at night to deposit gifts in the pots. Voodoo is practised in other countries of the Western Hemisphere that have large black populations, notably in Brazil

modern pharmacy that could induce a state of catalepsy or 'suspended animation'. Most of them, if mishandled, would be liable to produce brain damage. And whereas any modern hospital could quickly diagnose from the state of the victim what had happened to him, and which toxic substances had been adminstered, Haiti has few modern hospitals. And the ever-present fear of the zombie means that few if any peasants finding a wandering 'corpse' would willingly escort him to a doctor, where he could receive appropriate treatment.

So it might be that the belief in zombies is based on superstition, gullibility and straightforward fraud in which the 'zombie' is an accomplice. It may be that the 'zombies' encountered by some outside observers are no more than mental defectives. But it is also at least possible that evil men do have the pharmaceutical knowledge to simulate living death.

The law-makers of Haiti have, in fact, been alive to this possibility. Dr Villiers drew William Seabrook's attention to the Criminal Code of the country. Article 249 of the Code reads:

Also shall be qualified as attempted murder the employment which may be made against any person of substances which, without causing actual death, produce a lethargic coma more or less prolonged. If, after the administering of such substances, the person has been buried, the act shall be considered murder no matter what result follows.

Could it be, then, that the remote fields and hillsides of Haiti are even now being worked by 'dead' men and women, doomed to work on mindlessly until real death frees them from their enslavement?

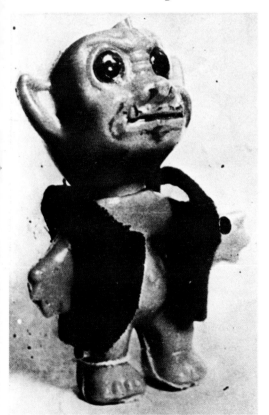

Black magic in the modern age. This Haitian voodoo image, a pin stuck in its chest to bring suffering and perhaps death to some victim, is a cheap doll made of plastic

Index